Y0-BRW-361

DATE DUE

GAYLORD

PRINTED IN U.S.A.

Red Multinationals
or
Red Herrings?

Red Multinationals or
Red Herrings?

The Activities of Enterprises from Socialist Countries in the West

Edited by Geoffrey Hamilton

St. Martin's Press, New York

First published in the United States of America in 1986

Printed in Great Britain

Library of Congress Cataloging in Publication Data
Main entry under title:
Red multinationals or red herrings?
   Bibliography: p.
   1. International business enterprises – Europe, Eastern.
2. International business enterprises – Europe, Eastern –
Case studies. 3. Industrial management – Europe, Eastern.
4. International economic relations. I. Hamilton,
Geoffrey.
HD2844.R44   1986   338.8′8947′01713   85–25102
ISBN 0–312–66656–X

Contents

List of contributors

Geoffrey Hamilton (editor) is Head of Research at the Institute for Research on Multinationals, Geneva, Switzerland. He has written numerous articles in the field of multinational corporations.

Malcolm R. Hill is Reader in Management Studies at Loughborough University of Technology, Leicestershire, England, where he teaches operations management and international business. His previous publications include *East–West Trade, Industrial Co-operation and Technology Transfer* (Gower, 1983) and a contribution to *Technology Transfer and East–West Relations* (Croom Helm, 1985, edited by M. Shaffer).

Peter Knirsch is Professor of Economics at Berlin Free University, where he holds the Chair for Economy and Technology in Eastern Europe. His fields of research cover many aspects of East–West international trade and technology transfer.

Jan Stankovsky is at the Österreichisches Institut für Wirtschaftsforschung in Vienna, Austria.

Eugène Zaleski is Research Director at the National Centre for Scientific Research (CNRS), Paris, France.

Foreword

At the heart of this book is an enigma. It concerns whether Eastern European and Soviet enterprises may properly be termed 'multinationals', and, even if we believe that they may be so described, how can we define the extent of their operations? The term 'multinational' brings to mind problems of control for the countries in which the multinational organization operates, and this relates to the definition of a 'multinational' as an organization manufacturing in one or more countries abroad. Excluding those few organizations such as Tungsram, which predated the Socialist system, Soviet and East European organizations do not manufacture abroad. Their activities are confined to trading and services.

The problem is similar to that of the whisky bottle — is it half-empty or half-full? Obviously much depends on the perspective of the observer. The contributors to this book have not tried to fabricate something that plainly was not there. The activities of Soviet and East European organizations account for perhaps 0.2 per cent of the private sector in the United Kingdom, for example, which is a very small amount, but this phenomenon has been growing since the late 1960s and we cannot tell how it may develop.

Investment in the West would seem to be anathema to pure Marxist doctrine, but it exists. Bukharin referred to monopolization as the symbol of capitalism, but it is today more prevalent in the Eastern bloc than in the West. The monolithic foreign trade structures of the state are monopolistic. In terms of foreign value-generating assets, they are limited more to sales outlets than actual production. One would not expect that they would evolve as the Western MNCs have done. This is unlikely because the entrepreneur is an unknown concept in the Eastern bloc, where mismanagement is a criminal offence, and the fulfilment of national plan targets is more important than incentives to exceed them. Prosecution creates a negative incentive in the absence of others, and leads managers to seek security rather than risk.

Another important difference in infrastructure is the availability of venture capital, which is only for certain national priority projects. It is certainly not available for foreign ventures. The growth of Apple

Inc. from its humble beginnings of the two founders operating from a garage to a large multinational firm could never have happened in the Eastern bloc. Another area of difference is that of Research and Development, where the Eastern bloc experience no conflict between state and enterprise. With perhaps the exception of soft contact lenses, the system in the Eastern bloc is less conducive to the rise of product innovations such as we have seen in the West. The better minds are directed more towards military and defence applications, while the East-West flow of techology has related most often to applications in the iron and steel, and mining industries.

Yet another obstacle to industrial progress in the Eastern bloc is that the concept of project management is still to be effectively implemented, for at present it is only to be found in Hungary and the Soviet Union. We might surmise that the advantage gained in overseas investment may be used to cirumvent the difficulties of the domestic market, but this would clearly be ideologically unhealthy no matter how appealing. Why then do they invest abroad? How do they undertake this investment? In what area? And with what return? These are the questions which this book raises and answers.

Dr Stanley Paliwoda
September 1985

Acknowledgements

Chapter 2

Malcolm R. Hill was assisted during the preparation of this chapter by a number of colleagues in the Department of Management Studies, Loughborough University of Technology, namely Mr J. D. Blake, Mr N. Coulbeck, Dr D. W. Cowell, Dr M. King, Mr C. P. McEvoy, and Mr J. Whittaker. In addition, much of the data of the most recent financial performance of British affiliates of socialist multinationals was collected by Miss K. N. Stables, a final-year student in management sciences at Loughborough.

He also wishes to acknowledge the continued provision of updated information on British affiliates of socialist multinationals from Professor C. H. McMillan, Mr P. Egyed, and Mr F. Cadieux of the East–West Project at the Institute of Soviet and East European Studies, Carleton University, Ottawa. Further information was also provided by the UK Department of Trade and Industry and the London Chamber of Commerce and Industry.

Finally, he wishes to record his thanks to those executives of British affiliates of socialist multinationals who were willing to be interviewed to provide information for the case study section of this chapter, and were willing to comment on previous drafts of the case studies.

The financial support for the research described in this paper was provided by the Institute for Research and Information on Multinationals (IRM), Geneva.

Chapter 3

Malcolm R. Hill was assisted by a number of colleagues during the preparation of this chapter. Preparatory work was carried out by Mr J. D. Blake and Mr J. Whittaker of the Department of Management Studies at Loughborough University of Technology, and Swedish company accounts and other financial information were obtained from the Swedish Royal Patents and Registration Establishment, Sundsvall, by Mr M. Bodin of the Department of Industrial Economics and Organization, Royal Institute of Technology, Stockholm, and by Mr P. A. Lawrence of Loughborough.

He also wishes to acknowledge the provision of up-to-date information on Swedish affiliates of socialist multinationals from Professor C. H. McMillan, Mr P. Egyed, and Mr F. Cadieux of the East–West Project at the Institute of Soviet and East European Studies, Carleton University, Ottawa. Further information was also provided by the Sveriges Riksbank, Stockholm.

Finally, a special acknowledgement is due to Miss K. N. Stables, a final-year student in management sciences at Loughborough, who provided valuable research assistance and analysis throughout the project described in this chapter.

The financial support for the research described in this chapter was provided by the Institute for Research and Information on Multinationals (IRM), Geneva.

Chapters 4 and 5

These chapters are an attempt to give as complete a survey as possible of Soviet and Eatern European investments in the Federal Republic of Germany and in Austria. Inquiries at Chambers of Commerce (*Industrie- und Handelskammern*) in the Federal Republic of Germany, at the Chamber of Labour (*Arbeiterkammer*) in Vienna, and at the Austrian National Bank, together with information from local trade registers form the basis of the study. It was thus possible to compile a considerably more complete and more detailed report of Soviet and Eastern European firms in these two Western industrialized nations than in the existing literature. Despite this broad empirical basis, the complexity of the material — in particular the fact that in both the Federal Republic of Germany and Austria certain types of enterprises are not compelled to disclose information — made it impossible to compile an absolutely complete list of local capital investments; nevertheless, the study is fairly comprehensive.

More regrettable than individual gaps in the list of such firms is the fact that it has only been possible to a very limited extent to gain information on specific details of these firms' business activities. The published sources available are extremely unsatisfactory. Interviews with experts from the business world who are well informed on the

practices of Soviet and Eastern European firms or holdings in
Austria and the Federal Republic of Germany did produce a
relatively uniform general picture; however, the limited research
funds made it impossible to proceed to case studies at the level of
individual firms. This would undoubtedly be an interesting field of
research, although the willingness of the firms in question to provide
information would probably set fairly narrow limits to the scope of
such a study.

The present study was conducted from 1982 until early 1983. The
search for material was completed in February 1983; essentially, the
information records the situation as of mid-1982. Leo Grosskopf of
Berlin assisted in collecting the empirical material for the Federal
Republic of Germany, and Dr Jan Stankovsky of Vienna collaborated
on the study of Austria. Mary Hess and Ruth Stanley of the Osteuropa
Institut, Berlin, translated the study into English. Peter Knirsch owes
thanks to all of them for their commitment and cooperation. Without
them, this material could not have been collected and evaluated. He
Takes sole responsibility for the analysis and interpretation of the material.

Chapter 6

E. Zaleski wishes to extend his thanks to Dr Malcolm Hill for his
useful comments on this chapter.

Chapter 7

Geoffrey Hamilton wishes to thank Eila Jounela, Economic Affairs
officer, Trade with Socialist Countries, UNCTAD, for her helpful
comments on an early draft of this chapter.

1   Introduction

Not so very long ago the common view of multinational corporations was of huge, privately-owned companies with their head office situated in the United States. Such an image was popularized in J. J. Servan Schreiber's book *The American Challenge* which recorded impressive post-1945 growth of American firms implanting themselves into European markets.[1] The 1970s, however, have witnessed a significant increase in the home bases of multinationals with more and more coming from European countries like Germany and France, Japan and even several developing countries like Brazil, Mexico, India, Hong Kong, Singapore and South Korea. The multinationalization of production and commerce has therefore become truly world-wide.

Set in this context of more nations acquiring their own multinationals, it may not seem so surprising to add to this list of 'new multinationals', enterprises from the socialist countries of the Soviet Union and Eastern Europe. Certainly, since the late 1960s there has been an increase in the number of enterprises originating in these countries with undertakings in the West and developing countries.[2]

This book attempts to examine the nature and extent of these companies to discover whether they are another expression of the multinational phenomenon: in short, whether these Eastern European enterprises are 'red multinationals'.

The organization and scope of the book

Are the foreign activities of enterprises from the socialist countries of the Soviet Union and Eastern Europe comparable with Western-based capitalist multinational corporations? The introduction to this book examines the concept of multinational corporation and how it has been used to describe the enterprises from these countries. It raises the question of whether these companies are multinationals or whether compared with 'real' multinationals they are no more than 'red herrings'.

There then follows empirical case studies by Malcolm Hill on these enterprises in the United Kingdom, Ireland and Sweden; Peter Knirsch on these companies in West Germany and Austria; and preliminary evidence by Eugène Zaleski on the role of these companies in developing countries. The conclusion to this study brings together all the evidence presented in the case studies to discover to what extent these enterprises are accurately described as multinational corporations. It also examines certain obstacles to these countries developing their own multinationals as well as making some suggestions for further research.

To the best of our knowledge this is the only study which has investigated in any depth the foreign activities of these business enterprises in individual countries. We are confident that it will provide an important supplement to the very impressive statistical work by the pioneer in this field, Carl McMillan from Carleton University, Ottawa, Canada.

Nevertheless, we are fully aware that much work remains to be done before we can reach definitive conclusions about these companies and their future role. For example, there is still a yawning gap in our knowledge about how these enterprises operate in the countries of the Third World. Moreover we have not examined these enterprises in every European country, selecting instead a representative group, i.e. United Kingdom, Ireland, Sweden, West Germany and Austria. It would have been interesting to compare the number and nature of enterprises from the Soviet Union and other Eastern European countries in these countries with, for instance, France and Belgium. But information for these countries proved, as with the other country studies, extremely difficult to obtain. Our hope is that the information we have managed to uncover will excite further study in this intriguing and so far underresearched area.

Data for these case-studies come predominantly from the 1980–1 period and in several instances 1979 statistics are used. Thus it could be said that the studies fail to take account of the world recession not to mention the political turmoil in Poland in 1982. It is true that the effect of these events, particularly the world recession of the late 1970s and early 1980s, caused a sharp decline in the growth of investments by the countries of Eastern Europe and the Soviet Union in the West.[3] None the less and partly because there exists so little systematic research on these companies, we feel that the information provided in these chapters is still relevant.

The United Nations Code of Conduct and Western interest in red multinationals

Why has interest developed now in this topic? First of all, interest has arisen in 'red multinationals' as a consequence of their recent emergence and rate of growth. At the end of 1981, more than 400 companies with Soviet and East European equity participation were operating over a wide range of activities in twenty-three OECD countries.[4] This represented a threefold increase in the number operating in 1970. Of course, Eastern European enterprises operating in the West have pre-dated this period. Tungsram of Hungary, for instance, was operating internationally before the Second World War. Nevertheless, COMECON foreign investments are essentially a phenomenon of the period since the late 1960s.

Another reason for this interest in 'red multinationals' is political and reflects the increasing tensions between East and West in the last few years. Eastern European countries along with the countries of the capitalist developed world and the bloc of developing countries known as the Group of 77 have been negotiating a Code of Conduct for Multinationals at the United Nations.

Discussions at the United Nations into the possibilities of concerted international action at regulating the multinationals began in the wake of the military coup in Chile, in 1973, and the revelations in the aftermath of an effort by ITT to enlist CIA support in a bid to oust the democratically elected government of Dr. Salvador Allende. A special United Nations Commission on Transnational Companies (UNCTC) was set up in 1974 with its own information and research centre to investigate the problem of multinationals and to coordinate work on a code of conduct. Developing countries supported by the bloc of socialist states sought in this early period to formulate a code of binding laws which would protect their economic and political sovereignty from the perceived threat of these huge companies. These demands, highly critical of Western MNCs, arose at the same time as the United Nations adopted the 'Declaration and the Programme of Actions on the Establishment of a New International Economic Order' and the Charter of Economic Rights and Duties of States'.

These desires on the part of LDCs to control MNCs through an International Code of Conduct waned as their economies were hit by the worst world slump since the 1930s. Efforts to control multinationals gave way to attempts to enlist their cooperation as governments sought ways of pulling their economies out of recession. Code discussions developed much more favourably towards the multinationals with the principles being implicitly agreed that a UN code would be voluntary and would be applied to government treatment of multinationals ensuring that foreign companies would not be discriminated against in favour of local firms.[5]

A further twist to code negotiations occurred at one of the latest sessions of the UNCTC, when the West argued that state-owned enterprises operating internationally should be included as transnationals and thus fall under the terms of a future code. Moreover, in the 1983 Session of the UN Commission on Transnationals (20–30 June), a proposal from a group of Western countries (Canada, Federal Republic of Germany, Italy, Japan and Sweden) requested the UNCTC to prepare for the 1984 Session of the Commission, a 'study on the activities of state-owned enterprises from both market and centrally planned economy countries conducting transnational operations and, in particular, on their activities in developing countries'. This proposal mentioned the increasing role in international economic relations of state-owned enterprises from both market and centrally planned economic countries, and the significance of such enterprises in the development process of developing countries. The proposal by the Western group of countries went even further to suggest that the UN Centre on Transnationals had not yet devoted sufficient attention to the activities of state-owned enterprises and that the Centre, therefore, should include these enterprises in all of its future studies on transnationals.

In order to support this motion, another group of Western countries (Canada, Netherlands, United Kingdom) had presented the Commission with a working paper on 'Direct Investment Abroad by Transnationals of the Member Countries of the Council for Mutual Economic Assistance (CMEA)' which gave an account of direct investment by Eastern European enterprises in the West as well as in Third World countries. Despite strong opposition from the socialist bloc countries, this working paper was published and distributed, as part of the Commission's report on the session. In addition, other Western countries (France, Federal Republic of Germany, Italy and the United States) had submitted a working paper containing proposals for the formulation of the preamble to the draft UN Code of Conduct on Transnationals. This working paper suggested that transnationals 'come from different categories of countries — developed countries with market economies,

developing countries and developed countries with planned economies. It encompasses all kind of corporations, whatever their nature
or method of funding and covers all sectors of economic activity'. The
reason why the West was pushing this issue was that the draft text for
the 'Third Comprehensive Study on Transnationals', conducted by
the UN Centre on Transnationals, had originally contained an
annex on socialist bloc enterprises. However, in the final publication
of this 'Third Survey on Transnational Corporations in World
Development', this annex, as a result of Soviet pressure on the
UNCTC, was omitted.

The Soviet Union and their allies strongly opposed any attempt to
have their enterprises and those of other Eastern bloc countries, put
on the same footing as privately-owned Western enterprises. For the
socialist bloc, the UNCTC was created to monitor only Western
Transnationals. Equally they claimed that the UNCTC was not
mandated to investigate state-owned enterprises from their region.[6]

In retaliation to this omission, the Western countries requested the
Commission to prepare a study on the activities of state-owned
enterprises 'in furtherance of the Third Survey on Transnational
Corporations in World Development'. At the insistence of socialist
bloc, supported by the developing countries this proposal was, after a
prolonged, heated exchange, voted down by twenty-six votes against
ten. Throughout these debates the Eastern bloc countries had
insisted that the Western claims concerning their own enterprises
were, to paraphrase them, little more than 'red herrings' to divert
attention away from the real debate about the West's multinationals.

Thus, given this actual political controversy which has effectively
blocked progress towards a UN Code of Conduct for multinationals,
the title of this study 'Red Multinationals or Red Herrings?' seems
fairly appropriate.

Existing studies on the 'red multinationals'

The most systematic and detailed Western research on this issue has
been done by Carl McMillan of Carleton University in Ottawa. He
supports the thesis that these companies are 'red'multinationals'. He
argues that their activities abroad are sufficiently analogous to the
foreign operations on Western multinationals to justify their inclusion in any consideration of global developments in multinational

enterprises. Thus he declares 'As a result, there appears to be no reason why they should be exempt from national or international regulation of multi-national activity'.[7]

McMillan's conclusion is based on a meticulous gathering of evidence of each East European investment in the West which he publishes and regularly updates in his East–West Business Directory.[8] While his conclusion tends to support the 'red multinational' thesis, his position should not be compared with the more sensationalist reporting of these companies which is regularly found in newspapers and business journals. A good example of this type is David Heenan's article headed with the claim 'The Russians are coming', in which he asserts that 'Moscow's multinationals ... oversee a growing intelligence network' and that the COMECON countries foreign marketing and manufacturing companies 'serve as a haven for spies'.[9] McMillan's own works dispute this view that the existence of these firms pose a threat to Western security. As he declares,

> considering the number of companies and COMECON nationals involved, the incidents of subsidiary personnel charged with illegal activities by host countries are relatively rare. An analysis of 76 instances of intelligence activities in the West, involving the Soviet Union and its Eastern European allies, reported in the Western press over a period of 12 years from 1970–81, revealed only 8 cases where persons attached to foreign subsidiaries were implicated.[10]

Moreover, McMillan concedes that most of the Eastern European investments in the West are trade-related, involving the setting up of agencies to market and service products in the West previously manufactured in the East. Nevertheless, taking as a definition for a multinational a company which owns units abroad, all the companies are therefore 'multinationals'.[11] Furthermore, he argues, most Western multinationals began operations in trade related activities to move eventually into foreign production. 'Red multinationals' which McMillan believes are still in their infancy will, he predicts, follow the same evolutionary path as their Western counterparts.[12]

Some have argued that the fact that these companies are state-run makes them different from 'multinationals'. But McMillan feels that their ownership makes no difference to their activities in Western markets. Just as the Western state-owned firm is similar to its private counterpart in local and international ventures so the state-owned

Eastern enterprise operating in a similar environment will bear many of the characteristics of Western multinationals, both state-owned and privately-owned.[13]

How should Western policy-makers respond to the activities of these 'red multinationals' in their countries? Like most commentators McMillan sees these 'red multinationals' as an offshoot of the rapid East–West trade expansion which took place in the 1970s. Just as it is in the West's interest to see such trade expand and prosper so this particular result of such expansion should be welcomed. Rather than posing any threat these companies 'bear the best current hope for the improvement in the structure and hence stability of East–West trade'.[14]

In a wider sense 'red multinationals' reflect for McMillan a greater flexibility on the part of East European policy-makers towards international economic relations. Instead of adopting the dogmatic Marxist-Leninist principles of two-world development and the irreconcilable conflict between capitalism and communism, this flexibility points to their growing awareness of interdependency in a single world economy less engulfed by irreconcilable class conflict and more challenged by the scientific and technological revolution. For McMillan these 'red multinationals' foster the development of a less rigid attitude amongst East Europeans towards international economic relations. It above all raises the socialist countries' stake in the order and stability of international markets and rests as an indication of its commitment to continued active participation in the international economy.

Moreover, the adoption of such mechanisms by the Eastern European countries reveals a more modern and innovative attitude to international economic relations than the one based on 'the cumbersome, centrally planned domestic production system'. If this trend is allowed to continue, capitalism will win some Eastern European adherents. As he declares: 'The practical training abroad of an increasing number of Soviet personnel services will improve understanding on the market system and possibly even instill some appreciation of its value'.[15]

Finally, the implantation of 'red multinationals' in Western markets will also benefit Western multinationals seeking to develop markets in the East. Red multinationals through their activities in the West can provide important services and linkages to Eastern markets for Western firms. McMillan's work was never destined to be used in the ideological skirmishes that have taken place in the United

Nations over the definition of a multinational. Nevertheless, Western delegations have used his work as evidence for their case that Eastern European companies should be treated as transnationals. Several Eastern European delegations that included distinguished economists have written attacks on such work and thus indirectly on McMillan's interpretation of his data base.

Several writers support McMillan's description of these firms as 'multinationals'. Both, Wilczynski and Zurawicki, use the term 'socialist multinational' to refer to socialist enterprises engaged in other COMECON countries.[16] Wilczynski states that in the mid-1970s there were around fifty state enterprises large enough to be classified as 'multinationals'. Zurawicki, while admitting that these 'socialist multinationals' are of recent origin, is enthusiastic of such developments. He maintains that these socialist multinationals are backed potentially 'by the total capacities of the whole productive apparatus of the CMEA countries . . . and that they . . . help to apply capital in the most productive way'.[17]

Such extravagant claims, however, are not shared by mainstream Eastern European social scientists who base their analyses of the multinational phenomenon on Lenin's classical account of the theory of capitalism.

This thesis links the export of capital with a particular monopolistic stage of the capitalist economy. The development of monopoly results in an increased mass of accumulated capital — through the break down of free market-price and profit mechanisms — with a simultaneous restriction on the scope for profitable investment at home. Capital export therefore becomes a necessity. As Bukharin wrote, 'thus the entire process drives capitalist economies and their interest tendency to monopolization'.[18]

This theory has notable weaknesses. Lenin was referring not to the export of capital in the form of direct investment but rather 'the immense accumulation of money capital' in a few advanced countries which was exported, in particular, in the form of international loans. Nevertheless, his theory is still used unchanged to describe the rather different phenomenon of foreign direct investment. Another weakness in the theory is that multinationals are to be found amongst small and medium-sized companies from non-monopolistic sectors of the economy — an occurrence which the theory has difficulty in accounting for. Nevertheless, for Eastern European social scientists, multinationals are huge capitalist transnational monopolies. The fact that one enterprise owns companies abroad is insufficient to classify it as a multinational. Indeed, as Valentin Shchetinin, Dean of the Faculty of International Economic Relations, Moscow Institute of World Economy and International Relations states, East European enterprises abroad are so different from Western transnationals that they represent an alternative to transnationals.[19]

The first major difference, according to Shchetinin, is that most of these companies are specifically market-orientated and promote the sale of goods produced in socialist countries to developed market economies. The functions of these firms include pre-sale servicing, warranty and post-warranty maintenance, provision of spare parts, etc. Thus their desire is to create trade opportunities, not the manufacture of products using local labour and infrastructure.

Secondly, these companies often exist in the form of joint ventures as a result of intergovernmental agreements. Unlike capitalist multinationals, 'this approach provides for full and consistent implementation of the basic principles of international relationships, such as respect for national sovereignty, adherence to national development goals and national cultural values and traditions, mutual benefit and non-interference in internal and international affairs'.[20]

Thirdly, the goals of these companies are not those of multinationals, since they are not in existence to make higher profits. As he says 'one cannot imagine that a Soviet partner, for the sake of higher profits, would support anti-popular and repressive regimes, or be involved in the operations of the military-industrial complex or the delivery of goods detrimental to public order, health or morality'.[21]

Thus, for Shchetinin, these companies share none of the negative characteristics of Western multinationals and, as a result, need not be considered as part of the transnational problem.

What are the multinationals?

Having looked at a variety of ways in which the term multinational corporation is used, it is now time to attempt a definition. What is clear from the preceding studies is that there is no definition of a multinational on which everyone agrees. International organizations like the Organization for Economic Cooperation and Development (OECD) or the International Labour Organization (ILO) have sidestepped the thorny problem of defining what a multinational is during the process of drawing up their respective codes of conduct for these companies. And as we saw, UN discussions about multi-nationals have been plagued by the same failure to determine a universally agreed definition.

For us a multinational corporation is best described by a number of its characteristics which from time to time have caused govern-ments and trade unions much worry and concern. These characteristics, to be described below, taken together make up what is usually meant when people talk of the multinationals, i.e. large undertakings which control a number of subsidiaries in several countries and whose strategy and organizational structure are conceived of globally.

The term multinational corporation is relatively recent. It was coined in 1960 by a little known American physicist who used it in a beneficient sense to describe the rapid spread of American firms overseas after the Second World War. As concern developed about the growth and spread of these corporations so the term 'multi-national corporation' lost its positive connotations and became rapidly a term of abuse. While the term is recent, the phenomenon of the multinational corporation is not. It has been shown that the multinational was as important to the world economy before the First World War as it is now.[22] None the less, the multinationals have grown apace after the Second World War and during the world economic crisis, when it might have been logical to expect firms to adopt a more cautionary approach to foreign direct investment, the process of multinationalization has accelerated quite dramatically.[23]

Characteristics of multinationals

Size

If one takes as a multinational a company which owns value-generating assets in more than one country, then most multinationals are in fact relatively small. According to UN statistics of 1976 around 20,000 companies could be called multinational using this wide definition. These 20,000 companies accounted for a total foreign turnover of US$ 670 bn. However, US$ 410 bn of this turnover was accounted for by only 422 of the 20,000 companies. Thus these 422 companies are those which are really being referred to when the term multinational is used.

It is often noted that multinationals are so big that they rival many nation-states as economic entities. For example, the sales of Exxon and General Motors are greater than the gross national products of countries such as Austria, Denmark, New Zealand, and Greece.[24] However, to argue that because a multinational's sales are greater than the gross national product of a nation-state the multinational is more powerful, is invalid. The power of a state and of a corporation are not comparable. None the less, this comparison does indicate a strength and influence in international relations which states cannot ignore.

Moreover the tendency seems to be for multinationals to become increasingly powerful. Under the impact of the recession and the growth of global competition there has been an increase in economic concentration with a few multinationals coming to dominate certain sectors like computers and automobiles. This process of industrial concentration has often occurred as a result of the takeover by multinationals of smaller national based rivals. Relevant here is the famous prediction by Perlmutter in 1968 which stated that 'by 1985 ... the world economy would be dominated by two to three hundred huge multinational corporations that would be responsible for the major part of world production and trade'.[25]

This prediction has been proved premature. Nevertheless, in some key industries a handful of firms dominate not only by the share of the world market but also in terms of ownership. Chrysler, Ford and General Motors, the big three American car giants, have a stake in virtually all serious European and Japanese rivals. In the high-tech sector (electronics, computers, biotechnology and robotics), large multinationals have often swallowed up national and smaller companies to establish their hegemony. Perlmutters' prediction may need revision only in terms of the date when the huge multinationals come to dominate world production and trade.

Technological sophistication

Multinationals tend to be at the forefront of technological advance. Their financial strength allows them to spend considerable sums of money on research and development. For example, the pharmaceutical multinationals spend in some cases up to 13 per cent of their turnover on research and drug development — a budget far and away superior to those of many public agencies.[26] A related cause of their retention of technological dominance over locally based rivals is their advantage in economies of scale. It is not surprising then that in the aforementioned high-tech sectors the multinationals are paramount.

Often, however, it is the smaller companies who make the initial breakthrough with a new idea, product or production process. But as the chairman of Philips recently stated:

> Once a new idea demands the integration of different technologies, then it is the large companies alone that are capable of translating that idea into products and systems suitable for the world market. Only large multinationals are capable of translating that idea into products and systems suitable for the world market.[27]

Integrated multinational production systems

Another important characteristic of the multinational is that the subsidiaries form part of an integrated multinational production system. The criterion against which the performance of a subsidiary is assessed is the contribution that investment will make to the group's global profits. For example, it may be necessary to have a loss-making subsidiary in one country to capture a market or obtain supplies of raw materials or semi-finished goods which would in the end significantly raise company profits. With this management goal in mind, a subsidiary is rarely considered independently but always as a part of a much larger whole.

The world-wide integration of a subsidiary takes several forms. A subsidiary may be responsible for a particular stage in the multinational production process. A prime example of this form of integration is the multinational motor-car industry which locates different stages and component-producing factories in different countries, the gear box in Spain, the engine in Portugal, the chassis in England and so on. This form of integration leaves little autonomy to the subsidiary. The latter is subordinate to the plans for the product as a whole which are worked out either by the regional headquarters of the firm or the parent itself.

Other forms of relationship between the subsidiary and the rest of the firm may allow for more independence. A subsidiary which makes a single product for its own market may in theory be more independent from this integrated multinational product system. But usually the multinational company organizes its subsidiaries in such a way that they become part of an international product division with authority residing with the central management of the division to fix product specifications, marketing arrangements, etc. This is not to argue that within this integrated multinational product system, the subsidiaries have no influence or leverage over the parent company. Only that the role played by the parent in shaping the goals of the multinational as a whole is considerable.

This centralized structure of decision-taking within some multi-national corporations has had political repercussions. For example, under pressure from the European Trade Union Movement, the European Commission has proposed a directive which would force the parent company to consult and inform the local workers of its EEC subsidiaries on important decisions affecting their livelihood. In response to such a threat the multinationals have been at pains to stress that their policy is to give greater autonomy wherever possible to local management and subsidiaries.[28]

Whatever the multinationals may say they are doing about the structure of their operations, certain factors make it difficult for them to carry out their intention to decentralize. The global nature of the economy and of competition has given more power to the centre in order to develop global strategies. Also developments in information technology allow much easier world-wide integration of production processes. The computerization and storage of information about the world-wide company operations occur at the centre giving more power to the parent company.

Why do firms invest overseas?

When asked why their firms set up factories and offices overseas, businessmen offer a varied number of reasons for this decision. These can be grouped under three main business strategies: market, supply and production rationalization strategies.

Firstly, in adopting a market strategy firms become multinational to avoid the barriers placed on their exports. Custom duties, import quotas, health and safety rules, are all employed to protect the national market from the competition of foreign imported products. Thus the firm sets up subsidiaries to manufacture on the spot products which were previously imported and in so doing ensures that their products are more sensitive to local tastes. Much of Japanese investment within the EEC is of this type.

Secondly, firms become multinational to ensure that their countries of origin are well supplied in raw materials like oil, tropical crops, copper and bauxite. The dominance of multinationals in this primary sector is under threat from the governments of less developed countries who have set themselves the task of taking over the control of their mineral, agricultural and energy wealth. In response these multinationals are moving out of the business of extraction and involving themselves more in the transport, processing and marketing of these raw materials. Countries, too, often retain multinational technical skills or managerial assistance even in those cases where national assets have been nationalized. For these reasons, the multinationals still exercise considerable control in the primary sector.

Thirdly, multinationals move overseas as part of a global strategy to reduce labour costs. Governments of less developed countries have been at pains in cooperating with multinationals in this strategy of production of rationalization. They have set up free trade zones where multinationals can hire cheap labour to produce components which are then assembled elsewhere. The free trade zones in South-East Asia, Singapore, Hong Kong, Taiwan and now China, in Latin America, Mexico and the Caribbean were set up to attract this type of manufacturing. Criticisms of these zones have centred on the poor working conditions of the employees (often young women), the prohibition of belonging to trade unions and the absence of any positive impact on the rest of the economy as a result of these free trade zone foreign investments.

Conclusion

This introduction has tried to outline the essential characteristics of the multinational corporation so that we can compare these with the foreign undertakings of enterprises from the socialist countries of the Soviet Union and Eastern Europe. Amongst these essential characteristics we have noted its tendencies to bigness, technological advance and, in the cases of manufacturing companies, its integrated multinational production structure. This is not to suggest that if the enterprises we will examine in the next chapters are not technologically advanced, huge, part of an integrated multinational production system or even successful high profit earners, then they are *not* multinational corporations. No one is expecting in this study to uncover an enterprise like a Ford, IBM or Unilever.

However, what one can legitimately expect if these enterprises are to be termed 'red multinationals' is the existence of these characteristics or some of these characteristics in embryo. We have noted how authors see these enterprises as being on a path which will inevitably lead to them becoming multinationals in the sense we have described above. It is to the evidence for this potential that we now turn to the country case studies.

Notes

1. J. J. Servan Schreiber, *The American Challenge*, Paris, Denvel, 1967.
2. Carl H. McMillan, 'Growth of External Investments by the Comecon Countries', *The World Economy*, **2**, No. 3 (September 1979).
3. See C.H. McMillan, 'Trends in East–West Cooperation through Direct Capital Participation', paper presented to International Economic Association Conference Budapest-Vienna, 8–12 October 1984. It is interesting to note that the recession has increased the process of multinationalization in Western capitalist firms. See C.A. Michalet, 'Multinationals: Reaction to Economic Recession', IRM Multinational Reports, Wiley, April–June 1985. If these enterprises from East Eurpe were like Western multinationals why should they not have reacted to the recession in the same way?
4. C.H. McMillan, op. cit.
5. For a fuller discussion on Codes of Conduct for Multinationals see Geoffrey Hamilton, 'The Control of Multinationals', *IRM Multinational Reports*, New York, Wiley, October–December 1984.
6. For an account of these discussions on the issue of 'red multinationals', see United Nations Press Release, Commission on Transnational Corporations, Tenth Session, 2nd Meeting, TNC/285, 17 April 1984.
7. Carl H. McMillan, 'Soviet Investment in the Industrialized Western Economies and in the Developing Economies of the Third World', *Soviet Economy in a Time of Change*, Washington, DC, US Government Printing Office, 1979.
8. Carl H. McMillan, *East–West Business Directory*, Carleton University/ Duncan Publishing, 1983.
9. David Heenan, 'Moscow goes Multinational', *Harvard Business Review*, May–June, 1981.
10. Carl H. McMillan, 'Soviet Investment in the Industrialized Western Economies', op. cit.
11. Carl H. McMillan, 'Direct Soviet and Eastern European Investment in the Industrialized Western Economies', Working paper No. 7, Carleton University, Ottawa, 1977.
12. Ibid.
13. Ibid. See also D. Buchan, 'Eastern Capitalists Strengthen Foothold in the West', *Financial Times*, 18 May 1983.
14. McMillan, ibid.
15. Carl H. McMillan, 'Soviet Investment in the Industrialized Western Economies', op. cit.
16. J. Wilczynski, *The Multinationals and East–West Relations*, London, Macmillan, 1976.

17. L. Zurawicki, *Multinational Enterprises in the East and West*, Alphen aan den Rijn, Sijthoff & Noordhoff, 1979.
18. Nicolai Bukharin, *Imperialism and World Economy*, Moscow, Merlin Press, 1972.
19. Valentin D. Shchetinin, 'Viewpoint: An Alternative to Transnationals', *CTC Reporter*, No. 16, Autumn 1983.
20. Valentin D. Shchetinin, op. cit.
21. Ibid., see also other works of Shchetinin on this topic, e.g. 'The United Nations and the Expansionism of International Monopolies', *International Affairs*, 8, 1981.
22. J.H. Dunning, 'The Organization of International Economic Interdependence: An Historical Excursion', Discussion Paper in International Investment and Business Studies, University of Reading, UK, No. 82, 1983.
23. C.A. Michalet, 'Multinationals: Reaction to Economic Recession', op. cit.
24. See N. Hood and S. Young, *The Economics of Multinational Enterprise*, London, Longmans, 1979.
25. H.V. Perlmutter, 'Super-Giant Firms in the Future', Wharton *Quarterly*, Winter, 1968.
26. R. Rigoni, A. Griffiths and W. Laing, 'Pharmaceutical Multinationals, Polemics, Perceptions, Paradoxes', *IRM Multinational Reports*, New York, Wiley, January–March 1985.
27. Dr. W. Dekker, 'Multinationals: Innovators in High Technology?', FT/IRM Conference, Munich, 24–5 April 1985.
28. See G. Hamilton, 'The Vredeling Proposal and Multinational Trade Unionism', Occasional Paper No. 11. Centre for Multinational Studies, International Economic Policy Association, Washington, DC, 1984.

2 Soviet and Eastern European company activity in the United Kingdom and Ireland

Malcolm R. Hill

Soviet and Eastern European foreign trade organizations and Western company ownership

Socialist foreign trade organizations and 'socialist multinationals'

In all of the socialist countries of Eastern Europe, the export and import of products and associated services are the responsibility of organizations accredited to carry out these tasks by the relevant country's Ministry of Foreign Trade. These may be 'foreign trade organizations' (FTOs) or 'foreign trade enterprises' (FTEs) directly responsible to the country's Ministry of Foreign Trade; or organizations (including 'foreign trade organizations') responsible to an industrial ministry, manufacturing enterprise or state committee having received Ministry of Foreign Trade accreditation. For the sake of simplicity, however, the term 'foreign trade organization' is used throughout this chapter to denote any organization within the socialist countries having the right to engage in foreign trade activity.

In general, an individual foreign trade organization is restricted to exports and imports of a particular product line, and duplication between the activities of foreign trade organizations is discouraged although apparently not forbidden.[1] It is probably easier to understand the functions of these foreign trade organizations by viewing them as export and import agents for a defined range of manufacturers. In some cases, they may be administratively separate from their customers as is the case in the Soviet Union, or they may be controlled directly by a manufacturing enterprise, as is sometimes the case in most of the other socialist countries. Foreign trade organizations are also frequently supported in their activities by a number of other socialist organizations providing various banking, insurance and other financial services, although these latter organizations may be also independently engaged in foreign economic activities in Western markets.

In addition to their usual foreign trading activities through imports and exports, several foreign trade organizations have engaged in investment and ownership-related activities in Western-based, or Western-registered, companies. Consequently, such organizations are sometimes referred to as 'socialist multinationals' or even 'red multinationals'.[2] The less pejorative term has been used throughout this chapter, although some researchers may question the use of the term 'multinational' in this context until evidence is produced of coordinated strategies of overseas manufacturing, servicing, and transfer pricing by these organizations.[3]

It is difficult to be specific about the sales turnover of foreign trade organizations, in view of the absence of any detailed published data. Estimates can be made, however, by comparing published data on the total export sales of a socialist country with the number of its foreign trade organizations. From such estimates, it appears that the annual average sales turnover of a Soviet foreign trade organization in the late 1970s was of the order of $1bn per annum, and varied from the $180m to $400m level for the remaining socialist countries. The exception to this was Hungary, whose average export sales turnover per foreign trade organization was less than $100m, but this was partly due to Hungary's policy of decentralization of foreign trade activities into a large number of organizations.[4]

The majority of the socialist countries carry out most of their foreign trade activities with each other through the Council for Mutual Economic Assistance (CMEA or Comecon). Consequently, the majority of the expertise resident in these foreign trade organizations relates to trade with countries having similar political and economic systems to themselves. Nevertheless, the expertise of these organizations in their dealings with the West is quite considerable, with about 20–35 per cent of each country's (except Bulgaria) export sales turnover being delivered to Western markets, rising to approximately 45 per cent in the case of Hungary.[5]

Ownership of Western companies

Foreign trade organizations carry out their export activities in a number of ways including direct sales, agency selling, and distribution through wholly-owned and partly-owned foreign-based companies.

Table 2.1 *Summary of foreign trade organizations' investment activity in Western-based companies*

Country	Total number of foreign trade organizations	Number of foreign trade organizations engaged in investment in Western-based companies	Number of Western companies in which investment has been made
	(1)	*(2)*	*(3)*
Bulgaria	41	11	20
Czechoslovakia	52	9	19
GDR	34	7	16
Hungary	72	19	42
Poland	50	26	101
Romania	45	19	28
Soviet Union	54	30	105

Source: Carleton *Directory*. 1979

Since this project is concerned with the latter type of commercial organization, it was decided to note the quantity of foreign trade organizations engaged in investment activities in the Western countries, as reported by the 1979 Carleton *Directory*[6] which was the most recent edition available when this research was commenced.

From Table 2.1 it appears that the respective socialist countries have operated differently from the viewpoint of ownership presence in Western countries. In the first place, it appears that Poland and the Soviet Union, and to a lesser extent, Hungary, have been far more active in the ownership of Western-based companies than Bulgaria, Czechoslovakia, and the GDR. For example, twenty-six Polish and thirty Soviet foreign trade organizations had invested in 101 and 105 Western-based companies respectively, compared with only eleven, nine, and seven Bulgarian, Czechoslovak, and GDR foreign trade organizations respectively, which had investment in some fifty-five Western-based companies in total. Hungary and Romania appear to fall into a middle range of ownership activity, with some nineteen foreign trade organizations from each country engaged in ownership activity in Western-based companies, with Hungarian organizations having investment in some forty-two such companies.

It is also apparent that further information can be obtained from some of the data shown in Table 2.1 and this is presented in Table 2.2.

Table 2.2   *Comparative ownership activity of foreign trade organizations*

Country	% of foreign trade organizations with investments in Western-based companies*	Ratio of Western-based companies containing Eastern investment, to number of FTOs engaged in Western investment activity †
Bulgaria	27	1.8
Czechoslovakia	17	2.1
GDR	21	2.3
Hungary	26	2.2
Poland	52	3.9
Romania	42	1.5
Soviet Union	56	3.5

* From columns 1 and 2, Table 2.1.
† From columns 3 and 2, Table 2.1.

From these data, it seems that a Soviet, Polish, or Romanian foreign trade organization has been more likely to engage in Western ownership activity than its counterpart in either Bulgaria, Hungary, the GDR or, particularly, Czechoslovakia, where in the latter case only 17 per cent of foreign trade organizations have investment in Western companies compared with 56 per cent in the case of the Soviet Union. In addition, it also appears that those Soviet and Polish organizations which had ownership in Western companies were more active in terms of the numbers of such companies, compared with their counterparts in the other socialist countries (see column 3, Table 2.2).

These average figures clearly need to be treated with caution, however, since they include some foreign trade organizations that had investments in one Western company only, and some others that had investment in more than twenty. Those foreign trade organizations with the most frequently recorded cases of Western ownership activity in the 1979 Carleton *Directory* are listed in Table 2.3.

It is thus apparent from Tables 2.1 and 2.3 that those twenty-four foreign trade organizations with investment in five or more Western-based companies represented almost 23 per cent of the 107 foreign

Table 2.3 *Foreign trade organizations having a high frequency of investment in Western-based companies*

Foreign trade organization	Number of Western companies containing investment
Dal (Poland)	21
Sovinflot (Soviet Union)	12
Balkancarimpex (Bulgaria) Ciech (Poland) Metalexport (Poland) Paged (Poland) Traktorexport (Soviet Union)	9
Carl Zeiss Jena (GDR) Sovfracht (Soviet Union) Soyuzneftexport (Soviet Union) Stankoimport (Soviet Union)	8
Hungarotex (Hungary) Animex (Poland)	7
Tungsram (Hungary) Avtoexport (Soviet Union)	6
Motokov (Czechoslovakia) Medimpex (Hungary) Agros (Poland) Polimex-Cekop (Poland) Chimimportexport (Romania) Energomashexport (Soviet Union) Exportles (Soviet Union) Soyuzchimexport (Soviet Union) Techmashexport (Soviet Union)	5

Source: Compiled from data provided in the index of the Carleton *Directory*, 1979.

trade organizations with investment in Western companies and had investments in more than 55 per cent of the named Western-based companies. The activities of these organizations are worthy of further study in their own right, but were thought to present too many difficulties of research procedure at the stage of the study described in this present chapter. For reasons of economy in research effort, therefore, it was decided by the present author to focus on the activities of 'socialist multinationals' in the United Kingdom, in view of the available information submitted publicly by British limited

Table 2.4   *Foreign trade organizations with investment in British-based companies*

Country of origin	Named foreign trade organization
Bulgaria	—
Czechoslovakia	Intersigma, Koospol, Motokov
GDR	Carl Zeiss Jena
Hungary	Chemokomplex, Hungarco-op, Hungarotex, Tannimpex
Poland	Dal, Agros, Hortex-Polcoop, Minex, Rolimpex, Ciech, Impexmetal, Polimex-Cekop, Agpol, Paged, Animex, Skorimpex, Metalexport
Romania	Chimimportexport, Navlomar, Romanian Institute of Atomic Physics
Soviet Union	Sovinflot, Soyuzneftexport, Raznoexport, Exportles, Sovfracht, Mashpriborintorg, Traktorexport, Avtoexport, Mashinoexport, Sudoimport, Techmashexport, Energomashexport

Source: Compiled from data provided in the Carleton *Directory*, 1979.

companies under British company law. This was supplemented by research on the activities of socialist multinationals in Sweden as outlined in Chapter 3 of this present volume, when it was found that Swedish regulations for the disclosure of information by limited liability companies were similar to those operating in the United Kingdom. Both of these studies, therefore, have been chiefly concerned with the gathering and analysis of data at the micro-level.

Ownership of British companies

Turning now to Soviet and Eastern European foreign trade organizations with investment in British-based importing and exporting companies, the 1979 Carleton *Directory* listed the foreign trade organizations shown in Table 2.4, as being engaged in that activity.

It can be seen from Table 2.4, therefore, that there were several foreign trade organizations with investment in British-based importing and exporting companies, which also had investment in five or more Western-based companies in total, as listed in Table 2.3. These were Motokov, Carl Zeiss Jena, Hungarotex, Agros, Dal, Ciech, Paged, Animex, Metalexport, Polimex-Cekop, Chimimportexport,, Sovfracht, Soyuzneftexport, Exportles, Energomashexport, Sovinflot, Traktorexport, Techmashexport, and Avtoexport. These accounted for almost 80 per cent of those foreign trade organizations with investment in five or more Western-based companies, as identified in Table 2.3. It is apparent at this stage, therefore, that Soviet and Eastern European investment activity in importing and exporting companies in the United Kingdom appears to follow a similar pattern to Soviet and Eastern European investment in the West as a whole.

A different pattern is evident for those Soviet and Eastern European organizations which are reported to have investments in Western-based companies, servicing foreign trade. These include:

Bulstrad (Bulgaria)
Zivnostenka Banka National (Czechoslovakia)
National Bank of Hungary (Hungary)
Hungarian Bank for Foreign Trade (Hungary)
National Savings Bank (Hungary)
Polish Ocean Lines (Poland)
Romanian Bank for Foreign Trade (Romania)
Ingosstrakh (Soviet Union)
Gosbank (Soviet Union)
Vneshtorgbank (Soviet Union)

In this group of organizations Gosbank and Vneshtorgbank are reported to have invested in five other non-British Western-based companies, and Ingosstrakh, the Hungarian Bank for Foreign Trade, and the Romanian Bank for Foreign Trade are reported to have invested in two others, but the remaining five other organizations appear to have invested in British-based companies only. This is probably a reflection on the importance of London as an international commercial and shipping centre.

The financial characteristics of British companies owned by socialist foreign trade organizations*

This section describes a study of the financial characteristics of companies located in Britain, containing investments from, and consequent ownership rights resting with, socialist foreign trade organizations. The companies were initially identified from the 1979 Carleton *Directory* edited by Bruce Morgan,[7] although updated information for their 1983 *Directory* was also provided by the Institute of Soviet and East European Studies at Carleton. Although it is clearly possible that this list may not be fully comprehensive, McMillan suggests in another publication[8] that Morgan's 1979 survey included approximately 90 per cent of all Western companies containing Soviet and Eastern European investment. In addition, the name of one further company was obtained from the London Chamber of Commerce and Industry and the names of a further six from the UK Department of Trade.

For the purpose of this study, it was decided to extract the following data, included in company annual statements of accounts as a part of the minimum disclosure requirements laid down by British law:

> name of company
> ownership
> turnover (above certain prescribed limit (£250,000 before 1980, £1m after 1980))
> profits before tax
> fixed assets
> current assets
> current liabilities

In addition, information was obtained on the year in which the company was established, or the year in which the company began to be owned by a socialist foreign trade organization.

The information obtained for sixty-one known companies for the two most recent years (1979 and 1980) for which data were available at the time of carrying out this research is presented in Tables 2.5 and 2.6 (and their footnotes) respectively. From this information it is

---

* For convenience, those British- and Irish-based companies which contain Soviet or Eastern European investment capital are referred to throughout the remainder of this chapter as 'affiliates of socialist multinationals in the United Kingdom' or as 'affiliates of socialist multinationals in the Republic of Ireland'.

Table 2.5 Ownership and financial information on affiliates of socialist multinationals in the United Kingdom, 1979*

Year estab-lished	Main business activity	Name of company	Shareholders (Eastern European)	% Eastern European ownership	Turnover	Profit before taxation	Profit after taxation	Assets			Liabilities		Total net assets
								Fixed	Current	Total	Long-term	Current	
Bulgarian investment and ownership													
1966	Travel agents	Balkan Holidays Ltd.	Balkantourist	50	no financial data available after 1977								
1966	Transport services	Balkan & Black Sea Shipping Co. Ltd.	Vodentransport	100	1,002,083	106,830	83,858	739,697	3,294,718	4,034,415		3,374,684	659,731
1967	Reinsurance brokers	European Reinsurance Brokers Ltd.	Bulstrad, Bulgarian Foreign Insurance and Reinsurance Co.	49	19,583	492	(103)	699	671,353	672,052		665,641	6,411
Czechoslovak investment and ownership													
1926	Glass marketing (technical)	Vitrea Merchants Ltd.	Transakta	100	743,953	196,647	90,147	31,644	1,144,541	1,176,185		690,493	485,692
1946	Travel agents	Cedok Ltd.	Cedok-Naradrie	100	—	(5,270)	(5,270)	34,839	47,079	81,918		21,917	60,001
1947	Crystal glass marketing	Henry Marchant Ltd.	Glassexport	100	1,067,924	44,495		148,689	812,724	961,413		793,666	111,747
1969	Marketing matches	Samaco Ltd.	Ligna	100	2,110,821	2,273	1,049	15,618	884,049	899,667		853,072	46,595
1928	Marketing food and agricultural products	Pilsner Urquell Co. Ltd.	Prague Nominees Ltd.	100	854,625	8,591	8,891	13,027	171,425	184,452		170,218	14,234

Table 2.5 continued

		Ownership					Financial information (£)							
									Assets			Liabilities		Total net assets
Year estab- lished	Main business activity	Name of company	Shareholders (Eastern European)	% Eastern European ownership	Turnover	Profit before taxation	Profit after taxation	Fixed	Current	Total	Long-term	Current	
1941	Marketing textiles and knitting machines	Omnipol Trading & Shipping Co. Ltd.	Transakta	80	490,769	75,793	32,405	21,860	602,383	624,243		337,045	287,198
1946	Marketing metallurgical products	Exico Ltd.	Transakta	83	11,189,405	95,651	40,385	35,417	3,551,444	3,586,861		3,055,367	531,494
1965	Marketing and servicing cars	Skoda (GB) Ltd.	Motokov	100	26,868,250	507,591	186,213	2,288,360	13,852,544	16,140,904		13,247,558	2,893,346
1967	Marketing and servicing pumps	Sigma Engineering Ltd. (This company is probably now wholly British owned)	Intersigma	100	431,548	35,219	35,219		546,751	546,751		340,270	206,481
1946	Transport services	Intrasped Ltd.	Cechofracht. Czechoslovak Ocean Shipping	100		13,292	7,592	14,564	145,289	159,853		145,952	13,901
GDR investment and ownership													
1963	Transport services	Deutrans (London) Ltd.	VEB Deutschfracht. Seereederei Rostock	100				62,463	9,497	71,960		71,958	2
1960	Travel agents	Berolina Travel Ltd.	Reisebüro DDR	100		(9,655)	(9,655)	92,574	63,706	156,280	106,746	58,563	(9,029)
1955	Marketing scientific instruments	CZ Scientific Instruments Ltd.	Carl Zeiss Jena	50	14,736,725	272,673		892,056	9,492,158	10,384,214		8,552,374	1,831,840

1968 Marketing consumer goods	Gebrinex Suppliers Ltd.	CZ Scientific Instruments (Carl Zeiss Jena)	100	621,351	(7,628)	(7,628)		425,286	425,286	420,041	5,241
1969 Marketing textiles and packaging	Unitechna (Service) Ltd.	Unitechna	100				3,291	3,148	6,439	5,439	1,000
1975 Marketing office machinery	Robotron Export-Import Ltd.	Buromaschinen Export-Import	100					4,535	4,535	7,635	(3,100)
1978 Marketing domestic electrical appliances (UK)	Heim-Electric (Import-Export)	Heimelektrik (Import-Export)	100					6,203	6,203	6,103	100
1964 Trade marks	Carl Zeiss Jena Ltd.	Carl Zeiss Jena, Stiftang	100	1,500	750	360		1,551	1,551	2,381	(830)
1970 Marketing vehicles and accessories	Transport Machinery (UK) Ltd.	Transport-maschinen Export-Import	100				3,420	19,921	23,341	22,341	1,000
1966 Marketing heavy machinery	Wemex Ltd.	WMW Export-Import					6,748	16,520	23,268	22,268	1,000
1978 Marketing furniture, toys and glassware	Hoglatex (UK) Ltd.	Holz und Papier	100					530	530	430	100

Hungarian investment and ownership

1976 Marketing fruit and vegetables	Central European Fruit Ltd.	Hungarofrucht	1		(3,697)	(3,697)	2,557	89,957	92,514	86,381	6,133
1969 Marketing textiles	T.H. Faulkner (Europe) Ltd.	Hungarotex	50		22,589	13,005	4,865	468,394	473,259	322,375	150,844
1972 Marketing household goods	James Griffiths Ltd.	Hungarco-op	50	411,879	(33,009)	(19,264)	232	660,260	660,492	652,486	8,006
1958 Marketing chemical products	London Chemical Co. Ltd.	Chemolimpex	80	5,268,117	32,508	7,888	10,163	763,285	773,448	682,193	91,255

Table 2.5 *continued*

Year established	Main business activity	Name of company	Shareholders (Eastern European)	% Eastern European ownership	Turnover	Profit before taxation	Profit after taxation	Assets Fixed	Assets Current	Assets Total	Liabilities Long-term	Liabilities Current	Total net assets
								Financial information (£)					
1968	Marketing leather fashion wear	Richmond Distributors Ltd.	Tannimpex	50	3,701,485	8,131	8,131	3,740	1,114,247	1,117,987		1,059,493	58,494
Romanian investment and ownership													
1968	Marketing chemical products	Arcode Trading Co. Ltd.	Chimimport-export	50	3,569,268	7,952	7,952	17,485	1,491,465	1,508,950		1,320,718	188,232
1974	Transport services	Navlomar Ltd.	Navlomar, Romtrans	100		66,910	38,293	2,014	133,743	135,757		56,435	79,322
1976	Marketing nuclear energy components	GEC Romanian Nuclear Ltd.	Romanian Inst. of Atomic Physics	50		5,721	3,052	—	79,129	79,129		3,005	76,124
1967	Marketing foodstuffs	Inter-Atalata Ltd.	Prodexport	50	3,848,323	122,819	57,379	663	583,405	584,068		425,503	158,565
Polish investment and ownership													
1974	Marketing metals and electrical products	FLT & Metals Co. Ltd.	Anglo-Dal Ltd. Impexmetal. Dal Ltd.	100	56,872,000	67,000	40,000	119,000	4,280,000	4,399,000		3,994,000	405,000
1978	Marketing tools and machine tools	Toolmex Corporation (UK) Ltd.	Metalexport, Pezetel (PZL)	100	1,169,838	(4,998)	(4,998)	176,839	2,165,097	2,341,936		2,212,403	129,533
1939	Marketing foodstuffs and household goods	Anglo-Dal Ltd.	Dal	100	4,198,417	9,017	31,076	325,250	654,399	979,649		821,632	158,017

Year	Description	Polish organization	UK company	%									
1976	Marketing shoes and leather goods	Skorimpex	Skorimpex Rind Ltd.	100	12,725,653	33,750	(13,727)	386,627	5,150,426	5,537,053	350,000	4,987,677	199,376
1976	Marketing machine tools	Metalexport	T.I. Polmach Ltd.	40	3,998,297	116,111	116,111	80,820	4,296,749	4,377,569		4,329,531	48,038
1976	Marketing	ARS Polona, Agnol	Polintra (London) Ltd.	50		2,065	1,719		13,491	13,491		4,686	8,805
1976	Marketing wood and wood products	Paged	Polish Timber Products Ltd	49	748,662	34,253	(7,362)	36,191	380,582	416,773		428,901	(12,128)
1976	Marketing chemical equipment	Polimex-Cekop	Polibur Engineering Ltd.	50	1,518,306	92,576	38,039	251,098	1,080,622	1,331,720		1,029,923	301,797
1959	Marketing chemicals	Dal, Salexport. Ciech	Daltrade Ltd.	85	693,097	101,026	49,020	265,605	387,924	653,529		433,370	220,159
1969	Book publishers	Interpress. Polintra (London) Ltd.	Earlscourt Publications Ltd.	5 / 85	571,502	12,873	12,873	23,082	259,976	283,058	55,640	240,685	(13,267)
1941	Transport services	Polish Ocean Lines. Polish Steamship Co. Polfracht. Central Fisheries Board. Ciech	Gydnia America Shipping Lines (London) Ltd.	100	—	10,381	4,616	230,213	1,361,498	1,591,711	28,500	1,410,734	152,477
1976	Marketing of meat products	Anglo-Dal Ltd., Animex	Ridpath Pek Ltd	50	21,960,998	73,462	33,462	185,799	2,919,946	3,128,151		2,777,003	351,148
1977	Travel agents	Orbis	Polorbis Travel Ltd.	100		26,120	14,838	47,527	281,742	329,269	193,185	95,062	41,022
1940	Shipping and forwarding agents	C.A. Hartwig S.A.	PSA Transport Ltd.	100	11,230,400	39,882	14,011	211,443	1,558,333	1,769,777		1,635,640	134,137

Soviet investment and ownership

Year	Description	Organization	UK company	%									
1974	Transport services	Sovfracht	Sovfracht (London) Ltd	100	1,122,329	421,336	167,924	228,330	765,459	993,789		631,050	362,739

Table 2.5 continued

Year estab-lished	Main business activity	Name of company	Ownership Shareholders (Eastern European)	% Eastern European ownership	Turnover	Profit before taxation	Profit after taxation	Financial information (£) Assets Fixed	Current	Total	Liabilities Long-term	Current	Total net assets
1969	Marketing consumer goods	Razno & Co. Ltd.	Raznoexport	100	5,284,300	40,102	35,228	435,258	1,674,257	2,109,515	119,002	1,637,964	352,549
1923	Marketing wood and wood products	Russian Wood Agency Ltd.	Exportles	>50	366,999	66,669	27,390	176,141	304,002	480,143		179,554	300,589
1959	Marketing oil and oil products	Nafta (GB) Ltd.	Soyuznefteexport. Russian Oil Prods. Ltd. Arcos Ltd. Anglo-Soviet Shipping Ltd.	100	720,812,000	742,941	742,941	4,683,132	100,260,934	104,944,066		99,696,938	5,247,128
1962	Marketing and servicing instruments	Technical & Optical Equipment (London) Ltd.	Technointorg. Mashpriborintorg. Moscow Narodny Bank	100	8,445,986	167,430	269,760	5,153,708	5,838,607	10,992,315	4,849,682	3,235,963	2,906,670
1969	Marketing and servicing construction and transport equipment	Umo Plant Ltd.	Traktorexport. Avtoexport. Mashinoexport. Techmashexport. Energomash-export. Sudoimport	100	3,704,279	(316,265)	(408,761)	1,317,401	5,520,822	6,238,223	3,523,589	4,288,046	(1,573,412)
1923	Transport services	Anglo-Soviet Shipping Ltd.	Sovinflot	100	215,261,021	176,203	1,000,613	999,788	14,350,297	15,350,085	358,292	12,933,454	2,058,339

| 1925 | Financial services | Black Sea & Baltic General Insurance Co. Ltd. | Ingosstrakh | 100 | 784,247 | 101,915 | 5,405 | 2,187,125 | 5,675,104 | 7,862,229 | 3,645,336 | 7,377,920 | (3,161,057) |

* The use of brackets denotes a negative value.

Notes:

1. The names of most of the companies listed in this table were extracted from the prepublication issue of the Carleton *Directory* (*East–West Business Directory: A Listing of Companies in the West with Soviet and East European Equity Participation*, Duncan Publishing, London, 1983). This prepublication issue was provided by the Institute of Soviet and East European Studies, Carleton University, Ottawa. The exceptions to this general rule are as follows: Cedok, Unitechna (Service) Ltd., Rohotron Export-Import Ltd., Heim Electric (UK), Transport Machinery (UK) Ltd., Wemex Ltd. and Hoglatex (UK). The first company was discovered by chance, and the names of the remainder were provided by the UK Department of Trade.

2. In addition to the companies listed in this table, BKC Impex Ltd. had been set up by the Bulgarian Balkancarimpex foreign trade organization in 1979, with 80 per cent Bulgarian ownership. To date, there have been no financial returns for 1979.

3. Financial data provided on two of the Soviet-owned companies require further explanation: (a) In addition to the fixed assets figure of £4,683,132 for Nafta (GB) Ltd., that company also had a secured loan of £252,302 in 1979, which was changed to £337,950 in a revised set of accounts for that year. Some financial researchers may report such a loan as an asset, but this author preferred to list assets exclusive of that loan. (b) Umo Plant Ltd. changed its firm of accountants at the end of 1979 from Deloitte, Haskins and Sells to Arthur Andersen. Following this change, the new firm of accountants subsequently revalued the company's assets and liabilities as follows: fixed assets £1,212,311, current assets £2,332,359, long-term liabilities £2,005,002, current liabilities £1,915,473.

4. The 1983 Carleton *Directory* also listed the following companies for which the present author, however, could find no information on ownership by a socialist foreign trade organization: Polonez, Elco Clocks and Watches Ltd., Global Watches, Fanuc Machinex Ltd., Pol Anglia Ltd., CET Plant Ltd. On a recent visit to Poland, however, the present author gained the impression that this latter company had been wound up and a new company (Cetco) formed by the previous Polish owners (Bumar) and different Western owners (Dresser Inc. instead of International Harvester). Furthermore, no financial information could be located on the following companies which were also listed in the 1979 Carleton *Directory*: Mutual Trade Ltd., Photographic Instruments (Elstree) Ltd., East-West Leasing Company Ltd., and Black Sea & Baltic (UK Provincial) Ltd., nor on Chimie Export–Import, a GDR-owned company listed by the UK Department of Trade.

5. In addition to the fixed and current assets shown for Black Sea & Baltic General Insurance, the company had other assets to the value of £6,521,277, mainly investments.

6. The financial information provided for Russian Wood Agency Ltd. relates only to nine calendar months during 1979.

Table 2.6 Ownership and financial information on affiliates of socialist multinationals in the United Kingdom, 1980*

Year estab-lished	Main business activity	Name of company	Shareholders (Eastern European)	% Eastern European ownership	Turnover	Profit before taxation	Profit after taxation	Assets Fixed	Assets Current	Assets Total	Liabilities Long-term	Liabilities Current	Total net assets
Bulgarian investment and ownership													
1966	Travel agents	Balkan Holidays Ltd.	Balkantourist	50	no financial data available after 1977								
1966	Transport services	Balkan & Black Sea Shipping Co. Ltd.	Vodentransport	100	981,959	171,376	102,283	705,230	2,912,417	3,617,647		2,917,453	700,194
1967	Reinsurance brokers	European Reinsurance Brokers Ltd.	Bulstrad, Bulgarian Foreign Insurance and Reinsurance Co.	49	22,215	(260)	(297)	34	991,417	991,451		980,464	10,987
Czechoslovak investment and ownership													
1926	Glass marketing (technical)	Vitrea Merchants Ltd.	Transakta	100	965,291	172,754	317,884	809,603	873,433	1,683,036		553,417	1,129,619
1946	Travel agents	Cedok Ltd.	Cedok-Naradrie	100	—	4,708	4,190	30,960	58,503	89,463		25,272	33,231
1947	Crystal glass marketing	Henry Marchant Ltd.	Glassexport	100	846,606	33,486	33,486	810,736	1,099,041	1,909,777		1,091,179	818,598
1969	Marketing matches	Samaco Ltd.	Ligna	100	2,434,005	31,158	34,202	19,571	963,082	1,002,653		921,856	80,798
1928	Marketing food and agricultural products	Pilsner Urquell Co. Ltd.	Prague Nominees Ltd.	100	983,757	958	657	15,329	176,677	192,006		162,745	33,118

Year	Activity	UK company	Partner	%	1	2	3	4	5	6	7	8
1941	Marketing textiles and knitting machines	Omnipol Trading & Shipping Co. Ltd.	Transakta	80	484,740	(1,289)	115,997	42,953	680,426	723,379	437,293	298,524
1946	Marketing metallurgical products	Exico Ltd.	Transakta	83	10,900,453	(92,792)	301,301	46,905	3,231,000	3,277,905	2,684,898	593,184
1965	Marketing and servicing cars	Skoda (GB) Ltd.	Motokov	100	19,612,932	(256,820)	(254,671)	2,311,269	12,433,204	14,744,473	12,134,141	2,610,332
1946	Transport services	Intrasped Ltd.	Cechofracht, Czechoslovak Ocean Shipping	100		31,790	18,510	19,354	256,465	275,819	243,153	32,666

GDR investment and ownership

Year	Activity	UK company	Partner	%	1	2	3	4	5	6	7	8
1963	Transport services	Deutrans (London) Ltd.	VEB Deutschfracht, Seereederei Rostock	100	(8,408)	(8,408)		60,697	7,713	68,410	68,408	2
1960	Travel agents	Berolina Travel Ltd.	Reisebüro DDR	100		14,032	67,229	77,549	144,778	106,614	55,511	(17,437)
1955	Marketing scientific instruments	CZ Scientific Instruments Ltd.	Carl Zeiss Jena	50	15,362,884			829,475	10,966,840	11,796,315	10,167,443	1,628,872
1968	Marketing consumer goods	Gebrinex Suppliers Ltd.	CZ Scientific Instruments (Carl Zeiss Jena)	100		724,571	18,978	14,438	302,669	302,669	282,986	19,683
1969	Marketing textiles and packaging	Unitechna (Service) Ltd.	Unitechna	100				5,799	1,920	7,719	6,719	1,000
1975	Marketing office machinery	Rohotron Export-Import Ltd.	Buromaschinen Export-Import	100				1,447	5,456	6,903	6,901	2
1978	Marketing domestic electrical appliances	Heim-Electric (UK)	Heimelektrik (Import-Export)	100					3,299	3,299	3,199	100

Table 2.6 *continued*

Year estab-lished	Main business activity	Name of company	Shareholders (Eastern European)	% Eastern European ownership	Turnover	Profit before taxation	Profit after taxation	Assets: Fixed	Current	Total	Liabilities: Long-term	Current	Total net assets
1964	Trade marks	Carl Zeiss Jena Ltd.	Carl Zeiss Jena. Stiftang	100	1,500	250	935		1,713	1,713		3,478	(1,765)

Hungarian investment and ownership

Year estab-lished	Main business activity	Name of company	Shareholders (Eastern European)	% Eastern European ownership	Turnover	Profit before taxation	Profit after taxation	Assets: Fixed	Current	Total	Liabilities: Long-term	Current	Total net assets
1976	Marketing fruit and vegetables	Central European Fruit Ltd.	Hungarofrucht	1 (previously 50)		2,331	1,731		10,676	10,676		7,814	2,862
1969	Marketing textiles	T.H. Faulkner (Europe) Ltd.	Hungarotex	50		5,590	4,090	6,300	418,078	424,378		272,904	151,474
1958	Marketing chemical products	London Chemical Co. Ltd.	Chemolimpex	80	6,558,176	25,957	65,787	15,723	614,698	630,421		513,746	116,675
1968	Marketing leather fashion wear	Richmond Distributors Ltd.	Tannimpex	50	2,070,415	16,060	16,060	26,182	1,850,156	1,876,338		1,960,378	(84,040)

Romanian investment and ownership

Year estab-lished	Main business activity	Name of company	Shareholders (Eastern European)	% Eastern European ownership	Turnover	Profit before taxation	Profit after taxation	Assets: Fixed	Current	Total	Liabilities: Long-term	Current	Total net assets
1968	Marketing chemical products	Arcode Trading Co. Ltd.	Chimimport-export	50	3,139,821	2,035	2,035	30,587	1,356,198	1,386,785		1,196,518	190,267
1974	Transport services	Navlomar Ltd.	Navlomar. Romtrans	100		16,674	10,714	4,788	156,443	161,231		91,195	70,036
1976	Marketing nuclear energy components	GEC Romanian Nuclear Ltd.	Romanian Inst. of Atomic Physics	50	—	8,544	3,467	—	79,525	79,525		8,082	71,443
1967	Marketing foodstuffs	Inter-Atalata Ltd.	Prodexport	50	11,851,658	174,847	82,516	5,597	1,305,850	1,311,447		1,075,251	236,196

Financial information (£)

Polish investment and ownership

Year	Category	UK company	Polish partner	%									
1974	Marketing metals and electrical products	FLT & Metals Co. Ltd.	Anglo-Dal Ltd. Impexmetal. Dal Ltd.	100	69,012,000	114,000	75,000	100,000	2,779,000	2,879,000		2,353,000	526,000
1978	Marketing tools and machine tools	Toolmex Corporation (UK) Ltd.	Metalexport. Pezetel (PZL)	100	1,102,341	(27,331)	(154,294)	151,797	1,758,605	1,910,402		1,940,163	(29,761)
1939	Marketing foodstuffs and household goods	Anglo-Dal Ltd.	Dal	100	2,339,535	(4,792)	19,921	367,340	291,525	658,865		505,457	153,408
1976	Marketing shoes and leather goods	Skorimpex Rind Ltd.	Skorimpex	100	26,183,695	44,354	77,504	465,523	4,068,045	4,533,568	350,000	3,902,017	281,551
1976	Marketing	Polintra (London) Ltd.	ARS Polona. Agrol	50		(2,155)	(1,802)		7,654	7,654		2,367	5,287
1976	Marketing wood and wood products	Polish Timber Products Ltd	Paged	49	657,810	41,832	11,430	31,049	278,395	309,444		309,404	40
1975	Marketing chemical equipment	Polihur Engineering Ltd.	Polimex-Cekop	50	6,289,528	10,066	209,203	219,774	1,140,859	1,360,633		1,048,770	311,863
1959	Marketing chemicals	Daltrade Ltd.	Dal. Stalexport. Ciech	85	1,200,847	56,363	34,097	265,474	483,247	748,721		454,468	294,523
1969	Book publishers	Earlscourt Publications Ltd.	Interpress. Polintra (London) Ltd	5 / 85	734,305	(20,275)	19,384	19,292	221,827	241,199	55,640	218,177	(32,618)
1941	Transport services	Gydnia America Shipping Lines (London) Ltd.	Polish Ocean Lines. Polish Steamship Co. Polfracht. Central Fisheries Board. Ciech	100	—	(12,639)	(10,210)	208,205	1,345,979	1,554,184	20,900	1,390,238	143,046

Table 2.6 continued

Year estab-lished	Main business activity	Name of company	Shareholders (Eastern European)	% Eastern European ownership	Turnover	Profit before taxation	Profit after taxation	Assets Fixed	Assets Current	Assets Total	Liabilities Long-term	Liabilities Current	Total net assets
1976	Marketing of meat products	Ridpath Pek Ltd.	Anglo-Dal Ltd., Animex	50	28,154,906	126,778	57,978	155,789	3,491,610	3,647,399		2,991,879	655,520
1977	Travel agents	Polorbis Travel Ltd.	Orbis	100		38,627	22,407	42,782	252,528	295,310	67,861	163,610	63,839
1940	Shipping and forwarding agents	PSA Transport Ltd.	C.A. Hartwig S.A.	100	11,337,914	(55,477)	(35,304)	199,304	1,592,383	1,791,687		1,698,112	93,576
Soviet investment and ownership													
1974	Transport services	Sovfracht (London) Ltd.	Sovfracht	100	1,634,266	768,266	379,200	235,175	1,932,987	2,168,162	20,196	1,718,485	429,481
1969	Marketing consumer goods	Razno & Co. Ltd.	Raznoexport	100	7,202,500	29,413	70,642	509,985	1,644,499	2,154,484	110,791	1,559,196	482,792
1923	Marketing wood and wood products	Russian Wood Agency Ltd.	Exportles	>50	454,840	(24,812)	(16,908)	341,759	149,218	490,977		163,881	327,096
1959	Marketing oil and oil products	Nafta (GB) Ltd.	Soyuznefteexport, Russian Oil Prods. Ltd. Arcos Ltd. Anglo-Soviet Shipping Ltd.	100	649,851,000	169,055	80,815	4,668,453	82,948,563	87,637,016		82,558,960	5,078,056
1962	Marketing and servicing instruments	Technical & Optical Equipment (London) Ltd.	Technointorg, Mashpriborintorg, Moscow Narodny Bank	100	5,806,392	(809,321)	(809,321)	5,171,068	6,480,477	11,651,545	4,849,682	6,678,335	123,528

1969	Marketing and servicing construction and transport equipment	Umo Plant Ltd.	Traktorexport, Avtoexport, Mashinoexport, Techmashexport, Energomash-export, Sudoimport	100	2,250,529	(484,363)	(323,056)	1,234,289	2,536,811	3,771,100	3,462,911	1,186,745	2,584,355
1923	Transport services	Anglo-Soviet Shipping Ltd.	Sovinflot	100	238,153,535	1,466,549	857,250	1,094,280	12,635,728	13,730,008	177,245	10,493,977	3,058,786
1925	Financial services	Black Sea & Baltic General Insurance Co. Ltd.	Ingosstrakh	100	1,181,364	21,818	12,630	2,140,594	5,896,008	8,036,602	4,308,674	5,920,141	(2,192,213)

* The use of brackets denotes a negative value.

Notes:

1. As no. 1, Table 2.5.
2. There was no financial information available for 1980 on the following companies which had been listed in Table 2.5: Sigma Engineering and T.I. Polmach (both of which were undergoing a change in ownership). Transport Machinery (UK) Ltd., Wemex Ltd., Hoglatex (UK) Ltd., and James Griffiths Ltd. Furthermore, the following companies were established in 1980 but no financial information was available for that year: Bulgarian Vintners Company Ltd. (100 per cent Vinimpex ownership). United Sterling Corporation Ltd. (50 per cent Ibernian (GDR) ownership). Fortschnitt Machinery UK Ltd. (100 per cent GDR ownership). Raznoimport (UK) Ltd. (100 per cent Soviet ownership. Raznoexport and Promsyroimport). A further company, Hibtrade, 100 per cent owned by the Hungarian International Bank, was established in 1981.
3. Financial data provided on two of the Soviet-owned companies require further explanation: (a) In addition to the fixed assets figure of £4,688,453 for Nafta (GB) Ltd. that company also had secured loans in 1980 to the value of £376,600. (b) The increase in current liabilities for Technical & Optical Equipment during 1980 compared with 1979 was caused by payment of a set of trading bills.
4. Black Sea & Baltic General Insurance had other assets, mainly investments, of £5,565,063.
5. The financial information for Robotron Export-Import Ltd. is for nine calendar months only.

possible to advance certain tentative hypotheses with regard to the size of affiliates of socialist multinationals operating in the United Kingdom, and also to identify apparent patterns of preferences for ownership amongst the different socialist countries.

Throughout Tables 2.5 and 2.6 attempts have been made to standardize the categorization of the financial data presented in the company accounts into each of the groups defined by the relevant column headings. Since each company has its own style of presentation of financial data, however, there may, as a result of recategorization by the author, be some differences between a specific company's own definition of the size of the relevant financial parameter and the value presented in these two tables. Such differences have generally been very small, with certain exceptions listed in the footnotes to the tables.

Dates of establishment of British affiliates

From the data presented in Tables 2.5 and 2.6 it can be seen that multinational activity is not necessarily a recent activity for the socialist countries, since three Soviet companies had been set up in the 1920s. Some Polish and Czechoslovak companies had also been established prior to the Second World War, and the activities of these companies were then continued by the relevant foreign trade organizations following the establishment of a socialist government

Table 2.7 *Dates of establishment of British affiliates of socialist multinationals*

Country of ownership	1920s	1930s	1940s	1950s	1960s	1970s	1980s
					Decade		
Bulgaria					3	1	1
Czechoslovakia	2		5		3		
GDR				1	6	4	2
Hungary				1	2	2	1
Poland		1	2	1	1	9	
Romania					2	2	
Soviet Union	3			1	3	1	1
Total	5	1	7	4	20	19	5

Source: Compiled from data shown in Tables 2.5 and 2.6.

and the nationalization of foreign trade activities. It is clear, however, that the major growth in the establishment of affiliates of multi-nationals occurred in the 1960s and 1970s, with approximately 70 per cent of the sixty-one companies being established during those decades and with some activity still continuing in the 1980s (see Table 2.7).

Turnover of British affiliates

Table 2.8 is a summary of the turnover of those thirty-four companies, out of a total of forty-nine listed in Table 2.6 for 1980, which provided data on their turnover. From Table 2.8 it can be seen that the total annual turnover from these thirty-four companies was at least £1.13bn. The total turnover figure for 1979 was some £1.15bn for approximately the same number of companies (thirty-seven), suggesting that there was little growth in the turnover for these companies from 1979 to 1980. Consequently, the average turnover per company was in the region of £32m per annum during those years.

During both 1979 and 1980, Soviet-owned companies alone

Table 2.8 *Total turnover of British affiliates of socialist multi-nationals, 1979 and 1980*

Country	Total turnover of socialist multinationals in UK, 1979* (£)	Total turnover of socialist multinationals in UK, 1980† (£)	Total turnover of socialist multinationals as % of British imports, 1980	Value of British imports 1980‡ (£)
Bulgaria	1,021,666	1,004,174	7	14,425,000
Czechoslovakia	43,757,295	36,227,784	41	87,812,000
GDR	15,359,176	16,088,945	18	88,127,000
Hungary	9,381,481	8,628,591	20	43,327,000
Poland	115,687,170	147,012,883	76	194,523,000
Romania	7,418,091	14,991,479	23	64,975,000
Soviet Union	955,801,361	906,534,426	115	786,176,000
Total	1,148,424,240	1,130,488,282	88	1,279,365,000
No. of companies	37	34		

* Compiled from data shown in Table 2.5.
† Compiled from data shown in Table 2.6.
‡ Figures for British imports are from: *Overseas Trade Statistics of the United Kingdom*, HMSO, 1981.

accounted for some 80 per cent of this total turnover, with Soviet-owned and Polish-owned companies together accounting for some 90 per cent. However, the Soviet Union and Poland were also the source of some 80 per cent of British imports from the socialist countries.

Some of the figures for each country reveals that the aggregate turnover figure is influenced to a great extent by the large Soviet figure, which in turn is influenced by the high value of the turnover for Nafta (GB) Limited — approximately £720m. If this turnover figure is discounted, the average turnover for the remaining companies reduces to approximately £11m per annum. Furthermore, the affiliates of Soviet, Polish, and 'Czechoslovak multinationals based in the United Kingdom appear to turn over an appreciable proportion of their respective countries' exports to the United Kingdom (more than 100, 76, and 41 per cent respectively), whilst in the cases of Bulgaria, the GDR, Hungary, and Romania the proportion is far less (7–20 per cent). Finally, since for one country at least (the Soviet Union) the total turnover of its wholly-owned British subsidiary is higher than total British imports from the respective socialist country, it can be tentatively concluded that these affiliates are engaged in other business activities besides the straightforward import of products into the United Kingdom. These activities probably include the export of products from the United Kingdom (in some cases this is explicitly stated), or overseas international trading activities operating from the British base.

Ownership preferences

The information contained in Tables 2.5 and 2.6 also provides some useful guidelines with regard to ownership preferences amongst the various socialist countries. In the first place, it can be seen that Soviet, GDR, and Czechoslovak foreign trade organizations appear to prefer to maintain complete ownership of their British-based companies, whilst Hungarian and Romanian foreign trade organizations appear to prefer to operate on a part-ownership basis (usually 50/50). Polish foreign trade organizations in turn appear to be equally willing to operate on either a part-ownership (usually 50/50) or 100 per cent ownership basis. It is also interesting to note, however, that those countries whose companies have a fairly high turnover in the United Kingdom appear to prefer, or to be capable of, operating with 100 per cent ownership (i.e. Czechoslovakia, Poland, and the

Table 2.9   *Ownership patterns of British affiliates of socialist multi-nationals 1980*

Country of ownership	Number of companies in UK having less than 100% ownership	Number of companies in UK having 100% ownership	Totals
Bulgaria	3	2	5
Czechoslovakia	2	7	9
GDR	1	9	10
Hungary	4	1	5
Poland	6	7	13
Romania	3	1	4
Soviet Union	1	8	9

Source: Compiled from data shown in Table 2.6 .

Soviet Union) (see Tables 2.8 and 2.9). Furthermore, Czechoslovak ownership activity in the United Kingdom appears to be fairly high compared with its activity in other Western countries (see Tables 2.1 and 2.9).

Size of investments

The size of the investments of the socialist foreign trade organizations in the United Kingdom can be estimated from the data shown in Tables 2.5 and 2.6 for 1979 and 1980. From the summary of these data in Table 2.10, it appears that the total fixed assets of socialist foreign trade organizations in British companies accounted for some £22m in 1979, and £23.5m in 1980. The total assets for these companies accounted for some £218m in 1979 and £196m in 1980, demonstrating that the majority of the investments in these companies were in the form of current assets, although this is a typical asset structure for trading and marketing organizations. The total net assets for these British affiliates during these years were some £23.5m and £26.5m respectively, which accounted for approximately 0.2 per cent of the total net assets of overseas companies in the UK private sector, and approximately 0.1 per cent of the total overseas investment in the UK private sector.[9] By these measures, therefore, it is apparent that the investment activities of socialist multinationals in the United

Table 2.10 *Fixed assets and net assets for British affiliates of socialist multinationals, 1979 and 1980*

Country of ownership	Fixed assets of British affiliates (£)		Net assets of British affiliates (£)	
	1979	1980	1979	1980
Bulgaria	740,396	705,264	666,142	711,181
Czechoslovakia	2,604,018	4,106,680	4,656,689	5,630,066
GDR	1,060,552	967,946	1,827,324	1,630,457
Hungary	21,557	48,205	314,732	186,971
Poland	2,339,494	2,236,329	2,124,110	2,446,274
Romania	20,162	40,972	502,243	567,942
Soviet Union	15,180,883	15,415,603	13,305,223	15,455,944
Total	21,967,062	23,520,999	23,396,463	26,628,835
No. of companies	46	43	54	48

Note: The 'other assets' of Baltic & Black Sea General Insurance, referred to in the notes to Tables 2.5 and 2.6, have been included in the net assets figure for the Soviet Union.
Source: Compiled from data shown in Tables 2.5 and 2.6.

Kingdom has been very small, compared with the investment activities of their counterparts from other countries.

Furthermore, it is also apparent that some 90 per cent of the fixed assets and some 85 per cent of the net assets owned by the British affiliates of the socialist multinationals in the United Kingdom were held by companies containing investment from either the Soviet Union, Poland, or Czechoslovakia during 1979 and 1980. Soviet-owned companies alone accounted for almost 70 per cent of the fixed assets of the socialist multinationals in the United Kingdom and more than 50 per cent of the net assets during these years. This suggests a proportionately high investment activity by Soviet foreign trade organizations, particularly in fixed assets, compared with their counterparts from other socialist countries.

Profitability

The final stage of this discussion is an analysis of the profitability of the affiliates of the socialist multinationals based in the United Kingdom, using the data compiled in Tables 2.5 and 2.6. From those data, calculations have been made of profit/turnover, profit/total

Table 2.11 Profitability of British affiliates of socialist multinationals, 1979 and 1980*

Country of ownership	Company	Indicators (%)					
		Profit/turnover		Profit/total assets		Profit/net assets	
		1979	1980	1979	1980	1979	1980
Bulgaria	Balkan & Black Sea Shipping Co. Ltd	10.7	17.4	2.6	4.7	16.2	24.5
	European Reinsurance Brokers Ltd	2.5	(1.2)	0.1	—	7.7	(2.4)
Czechoslovakia	Vitrea Merchants Ltd.	26.4	17.9	16.7	10.3	40.5	15.3
	Cedok Ltd.	—	—	(6.4)	4.7	(8.8)	12.6
	Henry Marchant Ltd.	4.2	3.9	4.6	1.7	39.8	4.1
	Samaco Ltd.	0.1	1.3	0.3	3.1	4.9	38.6
	Pilsner Urquell Co. Ltd.	1.0	0.9	4.7	0.5	60.3	2.9
	Omnipol Trading & Shipping Co. Ltd.	15.4	23.9	12.1	16.0	26.4	38.8
	Exico Ltd.	0.9	(0.8)	2.7	(2.8)	17.9	(15.6)
	Skoda (GB) Ltd.	1.9	(1.3)	3.1	(1.7)	17.5	(9.8)
	Intrasped Ltd.	—	—	8.3	11.5	95.6	97.3
GDR	Berolina Travel Ltd.	—	—	(6.2)	(5.8)	10.7	48.2
	CZ Scientific Instruments Ltd.	1.8	0.9	2.6	0.1	14.9	0.9
	Gebrinex Suppliers Ltd.	(1.2)	2.6	(1.8)	6.3	(145.4)	96.4
	Carl Zeiss Jena Ltd.	0.5	0.2	48.3	14.6	(0.9)	(14.2)

Table 2.11 *continued*

Hungary	Central European Fruit Ltd.	—	—	(4.0)	21.8	(60.3)	81.4
	T.H. Faulkner (Europe) Ltd.	—	—	4.8	1.3	15.0	3.7
	James Griffiths Ltd.	(8.0)		5.0	—	(426.6)	—
	London Chemical Co. Ltd.	0.6	0.4	4.2	4.1	35.6	22.2
	Richmond Distributors Ltd.	0.2	0.8	0.7	0.9	13.9	(19.1)
Poland	Toolmex Corporation (UK) Ltd.	(0.4)	(2.5)	(0.2)	(1.4)	(3.9)	91.8
	Anglo-Dal Ltd.	0.2	(0.2)	0.9	(0.7)	5.7	(3.1)
	T.I. Polmach Ltd.	2.9	n.a.	2.6	n.a.	241.7	n.a.
	Polintra (London) Ltd.	n.a.	n.a.	15.3	(28.2)	23.5	(40.5)
	Polish Timber Products Ltd.	4.6	6.3	8.2	13.5	(28.2)	104.580.0
	Polibur Engineering Ltd.	6.1	0.2	6.9	0.7	30.7	3.2
	Daltrade Ltd.	15.0	4.7	15.9	7.5	47.2	19.1
	Gdynia American Shipping Lines (London) Ltd.	n.a.	n.a.	0.7	(1.8)	6.8	(8.8)
	Ridpath Pek Ltd.	0.3	0.5	2.3	3.5	20.9	19.3
	Earlscourt Publications Ltd.	2.3	(2.8)	4.5	(8.4)	(97.0)	62.2
	Polorbis Travel Ltd.	n.a.	n.a.	4.5	13.0	36.2	60.5
	PSA Transport Ltd.	0.4	(0.5)	2.2	3.1	29.7	59.3
	FLT & Metals Co. Ltd.	0.1	0.2	1.5	3.9	16.5	21.7
	Skorimpex Rind Ltd.	0.3	0.2	0.6	1.0	(16.9)	(15.7)

Romania	Arcode Trading Co. Ltd.	0.2	0.7	0.5	0.2	4.2	1.1
	Navlomar Ltd.	n.a.	n.a.	49.2	6.6	84.4	15.3
	GEC Romanian Nuclear Ltd.	n.a.	n.a.	7.2	10.7	7.5	11.9
	Inter-Atalata Ltd.	3.2	1.5	21.1	13.3	77.5	74.6
Soviet Union	Sovfracht (London) Ltd.	37.5	47.0	42.4	35.4	116.2	178.9
	Russian Wood Agency Ltd.	18.2	(5.5)	13.9	(5.0)	22.2	(7.6)
	Razno & Co. Ltd.	0.7	0.4	1.9	1.4	11.4	6.1
	Nafta (GB) Ltd.	0.1	0.02	0.7	0.2	14.2	3.3
	Technical & Optical Equipment (London) Ltd.	2.0	(13.9)	1.5	6.9	5.8	(660.0)
	Umo Plant Ltd.	(8.5)	(21.5)	(8.9)	(12.8)	(19.4)	(18.7)
	Anglo-Soviet Shipping Ltd.	0.08	0.6	1.1	10.7	8.6	47.9
	Black Sea & Baltic General Insurance Co. Ltd.	12.9	1.8	1.3	0.3	(3.2)	(1.0)

* The use of brackets denotes a negative value.
Source: Compiled from data shown in Tables 2.5 and 2.6

assets, and profit/net assets for each company, and that information is presented in Table 2.11.

It can be seen from this information that few of the companies have performed well in terms of profit as a percentage of turnover, since of the thirty-four companies reporting both profit and turnover figures in 1979 and 1980, nineteen (or more than 55 per cent of the sample) yielded a profit/turnover percentage of 1 per cent or less in 1979, increasing to twenty-three such companies in 1980. Only seven of the companies reported a profit/turnover percentage of more than 5 per cent in 1979, this figure reducing to five companies in 1980, but it is interesting to note that two of the companies with the highest profit/turnover ratios (Balkan & Black Sea Shipping Company Limited and Sovfracht (London) Limited) were in the business of selling services rather than products.

When the profit margins (i.e. profit/turnover) for the thirty-four companies are compared with those for UK business as a whole (see Table 2.12), it appears that socialist multinationals in the United Kingdom appear to operate at comparatively low levels of performance for that business indicator. Approximately 80 per cent of the Soviet and Eastern European companies returned a lower profit margin than the median figure for that indicator for British merchandising companies during 1978–9, and 1979–80 (see Table 2.13).

Turning now to the indicator of profit/total assets, it is also

Table 2.12 *Summary of British industry sector profit margins 1978–9 and 1979–80 (per cent)*

Category	Lowest quartile	Median	Highest quartile
1978–9			
Manufacturing industry sectors	−0.7	7	12.5
Merchandising industry sectors	0.7	5	15.9
Services industry sectors	−4.9	8	32.5
1979–80			
Manufacturing industry sectors	−2.2	6.7	12.3
Merchandising industry sectors	0.8	5.1	12.1
Services industry sectors	2.3	4.5	24.7

Sources: Inter-Company Comparisons (ICC) Limited, *Industrial Performance Analysis: A Financial Analysis of UK Industry and Commerce*, ICC Business Ratios Division, London, 1981 edn., p. xi, for 1978/9 data, and 1982 edn., p. xiii, for 1979–80 data.

Table 2.13 *Profit margins for British affiliates of socialist multi-nationals during 1979 and 1980*

Year		1979		
Range of profit margins (%)	Less than 0.7	0.7–5	5–15	Greater than 15.9
No. of companies within this range	17	11	5	3
Year		1980		
Range of profit margins (%)	Less than 0.8	0.8–5.1	5.1–12.1	Greater than 12.1
No. of companies within this range	21	8	1	4

Source: Compiled from data shown in Table 2.11.

Table 2.14 *Summary of British industry sector profits/total assets 1978–9 and 1979–80 (per cent)*

Category	Lowest quartile	Median	Highest quartile
1978–9			
Manufacturing industry sectors	−0.9	9.3	18.9
Merchandising industry sectors	3.0	8.9	20.6
Services industry sectors	−3.2	9.0	25.6
1979–80			
Manufacturing industry sectors	−4.0	8.6	21.7
Merchandising industry sectors	2.3	10.3	19.5
Services industry sectors	2.2	8.8	23.1

Sources: ICC Ltd., 1981 edn., p. xiiii, for 1978/9, and 1982 edn., p. xiv, for 1979–80.

apparent that those forty-six and forty-three companies which returned this financial information for 1979 and 1980 did not perform particularly well against this measure either, although they appeared to perform better against this indicator than against profit margins. Table 2.14 presents a summary of the data available for British industry as a whole between 1978–80, from which it can be seen that the median figure of profit/total assets was of the order of 9–10 per cent for merchandising companies. From the information

Table 2.15 *Profits/total assets for British affiliates of socialist multi-nationals during 1979 and 1980*

Year	1979			
Range of profits/ total assets (%)	Less than 3	3–8.9	8.9–20.6	Greater than 20.6
No. of companies within this range	25	12	5	4
Year	1980			
Range of profits/ total assets (%)	Less than 2.3	2.3–10.3	10.3–19.5	Greater than 19.5
No. of companies within this range	22	11	8	2

Source: Compiled from data shown in Table 2.11.

Table 2.16 *Summary of British industry sector rates of capital employed (profit/net assets), 1978–9 and 1979–80 (per cent)*

Category	Lowest quartile	Median	Highest quartile
1978–9			
Manufacturing industry sectors	−1.5	15.8	34.0
Merchandising industry sectors	7.7	17.4	48.7
Services industry sectors	−4.1	23.5	64.1
1979–80			
Manufacturing industry sectors	−11.2	15.1	60.9
Merchandising industry sectors	4.2	19.9	54.9
Services industry sectors	7.6	19.4	56.8

Sources: ICC Ltd., 1981 edn., p. xii, for 1978/9, and 1982 edn., p. xiii, for 1979–80.

presented in Table 2.11, however, it appears that 75–80 per cent of the affiliates of the socialist multinationals located in the United Kingdom returned a profit/total assets figure of less than the British merchandising sector median during 1978–80 (see Table 2.15).

The ratios of profit/net assets for the companies presenting the requisite information (see Table 2.11) appeared to be highly variable, but on average did not appear to compare unfavourably with British companies in general. The median profit/net assets figure for the

Table 2.17 *Profits/net assets for British affiliates of socialist multinationals during 1979 and 1980*

Year	1979			
Range of profits/ net assets (%)	Less than 7.7	7.7–17.4	17.4–48.7	Greater than 48.7
No. of companies within this range	17	10	13	6
Year	1980			
Range of profits/ net assets (%)	Less than 4.2	4.2–19.9	19.9–54.9	Greater than 54.9
No. of companies within this range	20	7	8	9

Source: Compiled from data shown in Table 2.11.

merchandising sectors of British industry was some 17 per cent in 1978–9 (see Table 2.16) and some 20 per cent in 1979–80. Nineteen of the forty-six socialist multinational affiliates in Britain had a ratio equal to or greater than the median in 1979, and seventeen out of forty-four in 1980 (see Table 2.17).

It should be noted, however, that the relationship between current assets and current liabilities in some of these British-based socialist-owned companies does not always appear to be of a magnitude that would be expected from purely commercial considerations. In many cases, current assets are approximately equalled by the current liabilities, which frequently include substantial sums owing to the holding companies. The effect is that the net assets are of a smaller magnitude than would usually be anticipated, and hence the profit to net assets ratio is comparatively high.

Furthermore, it appears that those companies engaged in the provision of services (such as Sovfracht, and Balkan & Black Sea Shipping) have performed better on most profitability indicators than those companies engaged in the sale of products. These companies have also compared favourably with the median of profitability indicators for British service companies as a whole.

Finally, a high rate of profitability does not appear to be one of the primary objectives of the affiliates of socialist multinationals in the United Kingdom, but clearly they attempt to obtain a return on their

Table 2.18 *Financial characteristics of selected companies**

| Company | Financial indicator | Year | | | | | | Increase in sales | Increase in fixed assets |
		1975	1976	1977	1978	1979	1980	1980/1975	1980/1975
Skoda Cars Ltd.	Sales (£)	13,982.074	14,741.977	20,505.787	25,067.487	26,868.250	19,612.932		
	Profit (£)	753.360	137.577	183.522	168.275	507.591	(256.820)		
	Profit/sales (%)	5.4	0.9	0.9	0.7	1.9	(1.3)	140%	
	Fixed assets (£)	1,223.807	1,263.841	1,339.343	1,826.519	2,288.360	2,311.269		
	Equipment/fixed assets (%)	17.8	18.3	22.9	19.8	22.3	22.3		189%
CZ Scientific Instruments Ltd.	Sales (£)	6,993.289	8,742.593	9,434.606	12,579.627	14,736.725	15,632.884		
	Profit (£)	102.903	109.530	236.592	208.888	272.673	14.032		
	Profit/sales (%)	1.5	1.3	2.5	1.7	1.8	0.9	223%	
	Fixed assets (£)	170.969	168.843	259.596	345.863	892.056	829.475		
	Equipment/fixed assets (%)	38.8	44.1	39.0	51.0	31.3	27.2		489%
London Chemical Co. Ltd.	Sales (£)	4,575.330	4,598.067	6,252.247	6,084.006	5,268.117	6,558.176		
	Profit (£)	9.592	12.088	15.404	2.961	32.508	25.957		
	Profit/sales (%)	0.2	0.3	0.2	0.05	0.6	0.4	143%	
	Fixed assets (£)	4.995	7.600	10.102	8.940	10.163	15.723		
	Equipment/fixed assets (%)	100.0	100.0	100.0	100.0	100.0	100.0		314%
FLT & Metals Co. Ltd.	Sales (£)	2,115.973	15,005.845	34,065.813	35,969.000	56,872.000	69,012.000		
	Profit (£)	14.262	40.318	51.444	68.000	83.000	114.000		
	Profit/sales (%)	0.7	0.3	0.2	0.2	0.1	0.2	3261%	
	Fixed assets (£)	44.418	72.765	79.769	99.000	119.000	100.000		
	Equipment/fixed assets (%)	44.0	29.0	36.0	49.0	57.0	50.0		225.1%

Table 2.18 *continued*

Company								Growth	Growth
Skorimpex Rind Ltd.	Sales (£)	13,618,879	11,681,855	12,725,653	26,183,695			1980/1977 192%	1980/1977 384%
	Profit (£)	117,737	70,454	33,750	44,354				
	Profit/sales (%)	0.9	0.6	0.3	0.2				
	Fixed assets (£)	121,180	330,881	386,627	465,524				
	Equipment/fixed assets (%)	34.0	16.5	12.0	7.2				
Nafta (GB) Ltd.	Sales (£)	191,356,966	345,643,150	519,130,626	475,934,000	720,812,000	649,851,000	1980/1975 340%	1980/1975 316%
	Profit (£)	1,254,181	3,479,135	2,207,240	480,681	742,941	169,055		
	Profit/sales (%)	0.7	1.0	0.4	0.1	0.1	0.02		
	Fixed assets (£)	1,483,369	1,882,355	2,593,828	4,165,989	4,683,132	4,688,453		
	Equipment/fixed assets (%)	8.8	12.5	12.5	23.6	29.5	27.9		
Technical & Optical Equipment Ltd.	Sales (£)	4,548,168	5,615,088	6,858,277	8,445,986	5,806,392		1980/1976 127%	1980/1976 399%
	Profit (£)	67,854	297,647	99,840	167,430	(809,321)			
	Profit/sales (%)	1.5	5.3	1.5	2.0	(13.9)			
	Fixed assets (£)	1,296,595	2,770,203	4,218,742	5,153,708	5,171,068			
	Equipment/fixed assets (%)	7.2	3.6	2.3	24.3	21.8			
Anglo-Soviet Shipping Ltd.	Sales (£)	61,905,644	123,616,140	112,774,415	107,883,798	215,261,012	238,153,535	1980/1975 384%	1980/1975 91%
	Profit (£)	(242,692)	1,253,952	589,397	1,201,947	176,203	1,466,549		
	Profit/sales (%)	(0.4)	1.0	0.5	1.1	0.1	0.6		
	Fixed assets (£)	1,198,676	1,098,346	974,958	922,961	999,788	1,094,280		
	Equipment/fixed assets (%)	61.0	69.5	69.4	68.3	67.2	64.5		

* The use of brackets denotes a negative value.

assets sufficient to enable them to continue in operation. It is also necessary, however, to view these figures against a backcloth, for many companies operating in Britain, of general difficulties resulting from the international recession in general and British economic problems in particular. Nevertheless, it is probably safe to conclude that the socialist foreign trade organizations which own these companies do not necessarily view them primarily as a means of securing high profits but as important channels for the receipt of foreign currency.

Some further analyses were also carried out on a selection of the larger affiliates of the socialist multinationals located in the United Kingdom (see Table 2.18), from which it could be seen that whilst profit/turnover margins have remained stable at a low level, growth in turnover has usually been quite substantial. There is also evidence to show that the companies have increased their fixed assets, with some increase in equipment investment amongst some of the companies.

Soviet- and Eastern European-owned banks in the United Kingdom

A similar structure of banking has been established in all of the socialist countries of Eastern Europe except Czechoslovakia and Poland, consisting of a national state bank, an investment bank, and a specially created foreign trade bank. The main function of these latter organizations is to provide the necessary finance for foreign trade by:

> foreign exchange dealing;
> securing of import and export credits and handling of the associated documentation;
> making and collecting of payments.

In many ways, these activities are similar to the main business operations of the domestic overseas department of a British bank, and it is interesting to note that although there is no specific foreign trade bank in either Czechoslovakia or Poland, associated business functions are performed by two commercial banks, namely Zivnostenka Banka National of Czechoslovakia and Bank Handlowy w Warszawie. Both of these banks maintain a presence in London: the

Zivnostenka has a branch office and the Bank Handlowy also maintains a branch, both of which are licensed deposit-taking offices under the British Banking Act of 1979. The Bulgarian Foreign Trade Bank and the Deutsche Aussenhandelsbank maintain representative offices, whilst the Hungarian, Romanian, and Soviet foreign trade banks maintain correspondents but conduct all of their business from the head office in the respective home countries.[10]

In addition, there are three other banks which merit further description, namely the Hungarian International Bank Limited, the Anglo–Romanian Bank Limited, and the Moscow Narodny Bank Limited. A brief description of the activities of each of these banks is given in the following pages, whilst their financial performance is summarized in Table 2.19.

(a)   Hungarian International Bank Limited.   This bank, established in 1973, is a subsidiary of the National Bank of Hungary and a recognized bank under the terms of the British Banking Act of 1979. The activities carried out by this bank are as follows:

Bill discounting and forfeiting
Inter-bank deposit dealing
Forex dealing
Short- and medium-term loans
Loan syndications
Documentary credits
Trading in CDs (Certificates of Deposit)
Equipment leasing
Current and deposit accounts

(b)   Anglo–Romanian Bank Limited.   This bank is a consortium owned by the Romanian Bank for Foreign Trade (50 per cent shareholding), Barclays Bank International (30 per cent shareholding), and Manufacturers Hanover International Banking Corporation (20 per cent). It was established in 1973 and is a recognized bank under the terms of the British Banking Act of 1979. The main activities of the bank are currently documentary credits and short-term loans, although it is also intended to diversify into equipment leasing and ECGD export credits.

(c)   Moscow Narodny Bank.   This Soviet-owned bank was established in 1919 and has its headquarters in London, with branches in Beirut and Singapore. The scale of operations of this bank is far

Table 2.19 *Comparative performance of Soviet- and Eastern European-owned banks located in the United Kingdom, 1979*

	Bank		
Indicator	Hungarian International	Anglo-Romanian	Moscow-Narodny
Return on total assets (%)	1.1	1.1	0.11
Return on net assets (%)	20.0	25.6	3.3*
Value of deposits (£)	114,114,727	115,087,959	1,522,247,000
Value of loans (£)	83,423,034	99,787,147	1,189,801,000
	3,744,617†		
Capital ratio (%)	5.5‡	4.0	3.6
Loans/deposits (%)	76.0	87.0	78.0
Advances/assets (%)	69.0	81.0	75.0

* Profit after tax and transfers to reserves.
† Leased assets.
‡ Includes loan capital.
Sources: Compiled from *Banker's Almanac*, 1980–81, and the respective banks' financial returns.

greater than that of either the Hungarian International or the Anglo–Romanian, and in terms of total assets it is ranked at about 250th in the world banking league. The Moscow Narodny is engaged in all of the commercial activities listed for the Hungarian International Bank, as well as the following:

Sales of gold and bullion
Information and advice to the Soviet government
Training and education
Bond issues

The Hungarian International and the Anglo–Romanian appear to have an adequate return on both total assets and net assets. It is impossible to compute similar figures for the Moscow Narodny, since figures are issued after tax. The capital ratio for the Moscow Narodny appears to be fairly low for an international bank, and the loans/deposits ratio is at a fairly high level.

Case studies of British affiliates of socialist multinationals

This section is a descriptive account of the management policies and practices of five British companies which are either partly owned or wholly owned by foreign trade organizations from the socialist countries of Eastern Europe.

Selection of the sample

In order to obtain a sample an approach was initially made to those larger affiliates of socialist multinationals listed in Table 2.18, namely:

Skoda Cars Limited
CZ Scientific Instruments Limited
London Chemical Company Limited
FLT and Metals Company Limited
Skorimpex Rind Limited
Nafta (GB) Limited
Technical and Optical Equipment (London) Limited
Anglo-Soviet Shipping Limited

An introductory letter was written to either the Chairman or the Managing Director of each company briefly explaining the objectives of the research project and requesting their cooperation by a willingness to grant an interview to the researcher. London Chemical Company Limited, FLT and Metals Company Limited, and Skorimpex Rind Limited agreed to cooperate in the project, but negative responses were received from Skoda Cars Limited, Technical and Optical Equipment Limited, and Anglo-Soviet Shipping Limited. Although positive responses were also received from CZ Scientific Instruments Limited and Nafta (GB) Limited, it proved impossible to arrange an interview with the managing director of either of these companies within the time constraints of the project. A short account of the development of the latter company, however, has already been published by Goldman.[11]

In view of the extreme smallness of the sample of companies agreeing to be interviewed it was decided to contact another company located relatively near to the researcher's university (Toolmex Polmach Limited, (Narborough and Coventry)), and a further company reputed to be engaged in manufacturing activities (Ridpath Pek Limited). These companies readily agreed to be interviewed, thus completing the sample, which was interviewed in the following order:

London Chemical Company Limited
Toolmex Polmach Limited
Skorimpex Rind Limited
FLT and Metals Company Limited
Ridpath Pek Limited

All of these companies are owned by either Polish or Hungarian foreign trade organizations, but the willingness of these companies to be interviewed was considered to outweigh the possible disadvantage of any bias in national patterns of ownership within the sample.

Collection of material

During either late 1982 or early 1983 a visit was made to each of the sample companies for interviews with senior executives covering the following broad topics:

company activities
advantages and disadvantages of British company ownership compared with other more traditional methods for export marketing to the United Kingdom.

An explanatory sheet and checklist of questions was used for this part of the survey in order to provide a structured format for the interview, and the information obtained was then written in case study format. These case studies are presented in the following pages and relate to the times at which the interviews were carried out.

Case Study No.1: London Chemical Company Limited

(i) Company background

This company was established in 1972 as a joint Hungarian–British company for the sale of chemical products. The original ownership was 50 per cent Hungarian and 50 per cent British, but in 1979 it was changed to 80 per cent Hungarian (Chemolimpex foreign trade organization) and 20 per cent British (T.R. International), with an increase in capital. The company employs twelve people, ten of whom are British and two (the managing director and the marketing manager) Hungarian.

(ii) Company activities

The turnover of the company during the financial year previous to the interview was some £10m, with some £6m being accounted for in terms of UK exports to Hungary and the remaining £4m comprising Hungarian exports to the United Kingdom and third countries. The latter included the sale of propylene and C5 stream to Holland, which was more conveniently handled from a commercial viewpoint from London, but with cheaper direct delivery from Hungary to Western Europe. Such third country sales usually account for some 25–30 per cent of Hungarian exports, although in the previous year this figure was 50 per cent.

The exports to Hungary are handled on the company's own account for UK firms, whilst one third of the Hungarian exports are handled on the company's own account and the remaining two-thirds on a commission basis. In addition to these import and export activities, the company carries out distribution activities within the United Kingdom, and sometimes helps to bring about process licensing arrangements.

The company hopes to get more involved in distribution, based on its experience in the marketing of Hungarian-made tyres, which currently account for about 10 per cent of turnover. It has progressed from being a simple importer of tyres to a stockist able to provide a complete after-sales service (including claims and warranty) and capable of opening new accounts. It is interested in achieving similar goals of distribution capability for some ten new products.

The main objective of the company is viewed as the sale of Hungarian goods for hard currency in order to assist the Hungarian economy in the purchase of requisite raw materials and other products from the West. In addition, the company is also interested in the sourcing of some of these requisite Hungarian imports from Western suppliers. The company has managed to increase its turnover every year, and also to operate at a profit, which it considers to be no mean achievement in view of the condition of the British economy in general and of the chemical industry in particular.

In any joint-venture arrangement it is expected that a primary objective of the Western partner will be profit, both in total terms and in relation to turnover and investment. It was considered, however, that an 80/20 joint-venture arrangement prevented any conflict of interests arising from the different objectives of the British and Hungarian owners, since there was a clear majority in ownership and control by the Hungarian owners. Furthermore, the British partners are particularly interested in trade with Hungary, and hence ownership in the company at the present level of turnover and profitability is acceptable to them. In addition, it was extremely useful to the Hungarian partners to have assistance from the British partners during the setting-up phase of the company.

(iii) Advantages and disadvantages of ownership of a British company

Income, costs, and profits
In the view of the company, the volume of sales by Chemolimpex has increased as a consequence of the establishment of the company. On the other hand, the operating costs of the company are clearly higher than distributing through an agency, but the increased income from sales was at least at a high enough level to cover these increased costs. In addition, the income/cost relationships are such that sufficient profit has been created to facilitate growth of the company's assets and to enable the company to enter other business activities.

Ownership of the company was definitely considered to provide better control of pricing, compared with an agency, and also better control of selling. The company acts as sole agents for all Chemolimpex traded products except one, and also acts as sole agents for other Hungarian foreign trade organizations that now sell products which were previously sold by Chemolimpex. These products include items manufactured by the aluminium industry and the rubber industry.

Control of marketing
Compared with an agency, more influence has been possible by the company over the distribution of Hungarian exports, particularly the choice of channels and outlets of distribution. In addition, it is easier to establish the correct product profile in relation to market requirements. For example, the company is currently selling some three or four products in the United Kingdom manufactured by the Hungarian aluminium industry, and it is now discussing the

possibility of extending this range to suit its own product policy. At the same time, the company attempts to avoid competition with the four other Hungarian companies operating in the United Kingdom.

The company has its own advertising budget which it attempts to use in its best interests. It believes that its closer knowledge of styles and fashions in the market enables it to focus its advertising and promotional effort far more effectively. Furthermore, the company also provides advice to publicity agents in Hungary regarding advertising copy and the usefulness of exhibitions.

With regard to market information, the company sends monthly reports to Chemolimpex covering such information as general economic data, chemical industry activity, the company's own activity, and general market information from such sources as the *Financial Times*. The company considers its market information to be particularly reliable in view of its close day-to-day involvement in commercial activity and the fact that the information is more relevant since it is specifically gathered for foreign trade organizations in similar lines of business.

The managing director has limited scope in decision making, but can operate quickly within his terms of reference (for example he has some flexibility in prices, volumes, and deliveries). In addition, business transactions can be accelerated as a result of the managing director s knowledge of buyers and sources of supply, and effort can be accordingly focused on particular business deals instead of on the volumes of trade in aggregate which may preoccupy foreign trade organizations concerned only with meeting the quantitative targets of a foreign trade plan. As a result of the company's more focused approach, however, it is believed that conditions of trade result which are also generally more favourable to the foreign trade organization than selling through other channels.

Financial and legal aspects
The company was not unduly concerned over access to British equity capital and British sources of borrowing. The company usually generated its own finance for extra investment in such areas as extra warehouse space, salesmen, and advertising, and operated a normal bank overdraft facility of £50,000 which was not utilized very often. Furthermore, the company was not concerned over the protection afforded by limited liability in British law, since it was of the view that all liabilities would be met if the company ever decided to close down. The company selected a limited liability company as a convenient

vehicle for operation in the United Kingdom as this was the normal
type of company organization encountered in Britain.

Acceptance in the market
The company considered that its British name and UK location
provided a better acceptance in the market for Hungarian exports,
particularly where there may have previously been some prejudice
against purchasing products manufactured in the socialist countries
of Eastern Europe. In addition, the company found the general
acceptance of its London location to be useful when operating in
some of the Third World countries of Africa and Asia.

The company has found some resistance from some of its British
clients engaged in export to Hungary, since they consider that the
costs of the company's services may make their products less viable
in the fiercely price competitive Hungarian market. The company
can counter these claims, however, with the advantages of having
better contacts in the Hungarian foreign trade organization than its
British clients could foster themselves, and by the apparent
comparative cheapness of operating through the company rather
than either:

(a) establishing an office in Vienna or Budapest, or
(b) representation by a Budapest-based Hungarian organization,
     or
(c) frequent visits by salesmen to Budapest.

Access to British expertise
The company considered that access to British expertise was crucial
to its successful operation. It has received a great deal of benefit from
its British partners, particularly during the time of setting up the
company, and it finds that its ten British employees have a great deal
of local expertise to suit particular markets and buyers.

Case study no. 2: Toolmex Polmach Limited

(i) Company background

Toolmex Corporation UK, based at Narborough, near Leicester, was
purchased by its present Polish owners (the Metalexport and PZL
foreign trade organizations) in 1978, the company previously trading
as a subsidiary of Toolmex Corporation US. In 1981, the company

purchased T.I. Polmach Limited, which had previously been established at Coventry in 1976 as a joint venture between Metalexport, Daltrade, and a subsidiary of Tube Investments Limited, the latter being the major shareholder. Following this 1981 purchase the company was renamed Toolmex Polmach Limited, with Metalexport owning 90 per cent of the share capital and PZL the remaining 10 per cent.

The company is now divided into three main divisions, namely the small tool division, the industrial equipment division (which contains two subdivisions, one concerned with contracts and consultancy and the other with the sale of Polish diesel engines, generators, and aircraft equipment), and the machine tool division.

The company employs thirty-two people in total, including twelve in its Polmach machine tool division. Nine of these thirty-two people are Polish, five being employed in senior positions in the company's headquarters at Narborough and the remaining four in senior positions in the company's machine tool division at Coventry.

(ii) Company activities

The company is engaged in six main types of business activity, namely:

(i)   the import of Polish products into the United Kingdom;
(ii)   export from the United Kingdom of both Polish and British products;
(iii) tendering for project planning in third countries, sometimes on a joint-venture or industrial cooperation basis;
(iv) after-sales servicing;
(v)   the sale of Polish licences within the United Kingdom;
(vi) industrial cooperation activity with two British companies that involves the export of British components and imports of Polish finished products containing British components.

In addition, the company carries out the normal insurance, freight, and shipping activities associated with its major role as an importer and exporter of industrial equipment. No manufacturing activities are carried out in the United Kingdom.

The import of Polish products into the United Kingdom from the Metalexport range accounted for some £1.3m in 1980 and £1.2m in 1981. The current level of turnover is approximately £2m per annum, with just over half of this figure accounted for by the machine tool division. Re-exports have accounted for approximately 10 per cent of turnover annually.

Small tool division
The company's small tool division is engaged solely in the import of Polish-produced small tools into the United Kingdom. The product range includes precision measuring tools, hand tools, cutters and vices, carbide tools, and machine tool accessories. Some of these tools are also re-exported to third markets, but not into those countries where the company may act as a competitor to other subsidiary companies of Metalexport (i.e. France, Italy, West Germany, and the United States). The division also offers the usual replacement service for customers' returns, as well as a consultancy and sample trial service for its range of carbide-tipped or insert cutting tools. These tools are produced under licence from the Swedish SECO company and are currently being introduced into service in J.C.B. and Massey-Ferguson-Perkins Limited.

Industrial equipment division: contracts, special projects, and consultancy subdivision

(a) Exports to Poland.   This subdivision has acted as a representative for a number of British companies engaged in the export to Poland of machine tools and associated production equipment. The subdivision has excellent contacts with Metalexport's buying offices through the company's Warsaw office and can ensure that its British principals' quotations receive top priority. In addition, the subdivision can arrange for the receipt of Polish enquiries by their British principals, advise on the preparation of quotations, arrange meetings with Polish buyers, and generally expedite the on-site installation and acceptance stages.

The companies represented in this way include such well-established machine tool exporters as Matrix-Churchill, Wadkin, Browne and Sharpe, Sykes, Precision Gear, M. and T. Chemicals, and John Brown Industries. Most of these firms have exported equipment for the large 'Ursus' tractor project which is being carried out through an industrial cooperation agreement with Massey-Ferguson-Perkins Limited (MFP). Several small firms were also recommended as suppliers by MFP, and were originally approached by this subdivision of Toolmex Polmach as potential customers for its export services. Some of these small firms had never exported before being approached by Toolmex Polmach.

The company receives income for these services in two ways: retainer fees are paid by some firms for the subdivision's representational activities, whilst others pay a commission on the contracts obtained. This varies between 0.5 and 1.5 per cent of the value of the contract signed between the British companies and Metalexport as principals, and may only commence above a certain threshhold level of retainer fee. In addition the company exports other products on its own account to Poland on a cash basis as and when these are required at short notice by Polish buyers.

The total value of exports to Poland handled by the company was some £22m in 1980 and some £12m in 1981, the majority of these British exports being for equipment purchased for use in the 'Ursus' factory project. These activities accounted for an income of some £120,000 in 1980 and £61,000 in 1981. The financial objective of these activities has not necessarily been one of profit maximization but of covering the costs associated with these activities, namely the services of commercial engineers and associated secretaries, telexes, and administrative overheads. In general, it has been possible to cover costs by appropriate matching of staffing levels to business demand, and some profits have also been generated. These activities are, therefore, viewed by the company as being:

(a) beneficial to the British firms concerned because of the representational services received;
(b) useful to Metalexport's buying office since the company will always attempt to locate firms which are technically competent and commercially reliable;
(c) economically advantageous to the company in view of the income received.

A final aspect of the subdivision's activities relating to imports into Poland are its representational responsibilities for some of Metalexport's purchasing activities related to the 'Ursus' project. These tasks include the monitoring of quotations related to the purchase of plant, and the arrangement of appropriate discussions and tests. Clearly the company is in a more advantageous geographical position than Metalexport's Warsaw office to carry out these tasks, and an appropriate commission is received from Metalexport's buying office to cover the costs of these activities.

(b) Project contracting services. This subdivision of the company offers a contracting service for projects in third countries, and has tendered for the supply of Polish-manufactured equipment to third countries through joint-venture projects in which British companies are project leaders.

(c) Sale of licences. The company acts for Polservice on an agency basis and has sold licences accordingly. This activity is carried out largely by the contracts and consultancy subdivision.

(d) Industrial cooperation. The company has commenced industrial cooperation activities with two Western firms, namely Liftec S.A. of Switzerland, which is the holding company for Lansing Bagnall, the British manufacturer of fork-lift trucks, and M. & T. Chemicals Limited, a Birmingham-based manufacturer of electroplating equipment. In both cases, the agreement has been signed between the Western firms and Metalexport, with the company acting as the Western firms' representative through its contracts and consultancy subdivisions.

In the case of the Liftec agreement, Lansing Bagnall supplies some ready-made products and components and the Polish partner produces other components (mainly of the labour-intensive variety) and provides after-sales service in Poland through its Warsaw office. Lansing Bagnall buys finished trucks made using these British-made and Polish-made components from its Polish partner, which are then distributed through its own network. Some 300 trucks have been imported into the United Kingdom over the past year.

A similar arrangement exists with M. & T. Chemicals, with Polish-made filters and centrifuges built from UK and Polish-made components being imported by the British company for use in its electroplating equipment.

Industrial equipment division: diesel engines and aviation products subdivision

This subdivision of the company is concerned with the import into the United Kingdom of Polish diesel engines produced to Leyland and Rheinstal and Henschel licences, power generators, the PZL range of gliders and light aircraft, and electrical vehicles for factory materials handling and golf buggies. In addition, the subdivision provides an after-sales service for its product range and, very occasionally, also purchases British products, chiefly to promote imports of Polish products.

The subdivision operates differentiated methods of marketing according to the product under consideration. For the diesel engines and generators it acts as importers, although recent conditions in the British market have caused the bulk of its current sales to be mainly spares. In the case of electrical vehicles it acts as stockists, operating through one main distributor for whom it imports, holds stocks, and arranges finance. In the case of gliders and light aircraft it acts as agent and representative for the Polish exporter, with a UK company acting as the main importer.

Machine tool division

The company's machine tool division is primarily engaged in the import of Polish-built machine tools into the United Kingdom, although it also uses the UK base for re-exporting to third countries (such as Taiwan). In addition, the division is attempting to establish itself as a merchant for certain makes of British and West German machine tools which can complement its existing product range.

The other major activity carried out by the division is that of servicing, which is considered of crucial importance for the technical products sold, of which there are 180 types. The company provides guarantee service for new machines, as well as the normal after-sales service facilities. In addition, a reconditioning service is now being offered, since Metalexport has sold 7,000 Polish machines to the British market over the past twenty-five years.

(iii)   Advantages and disadvantages of company ownership

Income, costs, and profits

The company considers that compared with other forms of business organization, ownership of a British company presents the opportunity to increase sales and consequent income. General economic recession, and the depression of the British economy in particular, however, have prevented the company's divisions from expanding their volume of sales, but the company considers that the achievement of their present levels of sales in the current economic climate indicates a comparatively successful business operation.

Clearly, operating costs are higher than selling through an agency, and profitability is consequently dependent upon market conditions: if the market improves, leading to better turnover and prices, the profits should consequently increase. Although the company considers that its priority objective is a high turnover of Polish products in British and third markets in order to obtain hard currency for its owners, it is also considered necessary to make adequate profits to maintain operations and expand. These profits are also required to cover such expenses as the costs of purchase of special components and accessories from Western sources required for the sale of Polish machine tools to certain markets. It was the company's view that the company's performance could not be compared with sales through an agency, since many of its activities related to exports to Poland and to selling in the United Kingdom through distributors and dealers.

Control of marketing

Ownership of a company provides better control over pricing and selling, in view of the closer contact with British and Polish customers and suppliers alike, than could be obtained through other means of business organization. Permanent location in the United Kingdom also means that the company can easily check the financial position of British suppliers and distributors and consequently select the most stable sources of supply and channels of distribution. The better control of distribution and selling is considered to be critical to the successful operation of the company's small tool and machine tool divisions.

For small tools, the company believes that it would be impossible to service the British market satisfactorily directly from Poland in view of the peculiar features of this market. These can be summarized as a large number of small distributors (approximately 250) requiring both metric- and imperial-sized tools, and these distributors can be served far better as a result of clearer understanding of their needs through closer personal contact. In order to service the British small tool market adequately, it is necessary to hold a broad range of stocks from which the company can service an order within two to three days using the Post Office or contract carriers. At present, neither agents nor distributors are currently willing to hold stock in the United Kingdom and so it is even more necessary for the Polish exporters to have a UK location to stock their products, particularly as, in common with other sources of British small tool imports, delivery lead times may extend to some three to four months for some items.

The company also considers that it can analyse small tool market prices far better than by relying on agencies, obtaining better market information through the services of its own salesmen, and access to published market reports and competitors' price lists. The company also has better control over selling through the employment of its own salesmen and the implementation of its own computerized system for stock control and sales and customer information.

For the machine tool division, the control of selling and distribution is much better than selling through an agency, since the division has selected its own salesmen and established its own channels of distribution. The British salesmen are clearly more adept at handling the commercial and some of the technical aspects of the sale, but the presence of a Polish Technical Director and the availability of Polish engineers has led to excellent technical support based on detailed knowledge of the product. This is particularly important in the case of machine tools, where detailed knowledge is required of the product's design, manufacture, and capability. In addition, since its formation the division has made great efforts to create an adequate and reliable after-sales service, and as a result of customer satisfaction it can now sell service in a confident manner.

The company's better control over distribution now means that it can exert more influence over the channels through which the machines are sold. For example, instead of making all sales from the company's premises in Coventry, it may be better to use merchants to sell standard machines (with arrangements made to provide appropriate stocks) and to use the Coventry-based salesmen to concentrate on the sale of more specialized and sophisticated machines.

Advertising, promotion, and decision making
All divisions of the company concerned with the import of Polish products into the United Kingdom considered that the control of advertising and promotion has generally been better than through agency selling. This is a consequence of the company being in a position to enlist good supplier support, with appropriate advertisements and promotional literature. These advertisements can then be focused through the use of the most appropriate trade journals. In addition, the company's machine tool division has been in a good position to collect specific market information, especially that of a technical nature, in view of Polish technical staff being located in the United Kingdom. As a consequence of there being advantages in all of the factors listed here, it was considered by all divisions of the

company that decision making was generally faster as compared with agency selling.

Financial and legal aspects

Theoretically, the company has access to British sources of equity capital and borrowing, but in practice they have seldom been used except occasionally to finance stocks. It was also found to be easier to arrange finance, credit, and ECGD cover for those British exports to Poland which were handled by the company, as a consequence of being able to arrange meetings and build up good relationships with the appropriate British financial institutions.

A limited liability form of business organization was selected to facilitate general ease of trading and defined taxation responsibilities. Furthermore, as the company regards its good reputation as one of its greatest assets, its corporate status helps to reinforce a general view of the company's commercial seriousness amongst the British business community. The company also preferred the wholly Polish-owned corporate organization to a joint-venture arrangement in which the Polish owners may have limited ownership and control rights but be comparatively large creditors.

Acceptance in the market

The company has built up a good reputation in the market as a consequence of its technical service through factory-trained personnel, communication with Polish enterprises and factories, and access to British expertise. The company is of the view that these activities can be carried out more effectively by a wholly-owned corporate entity located in the United Kingdom rather than through the medium of an agency. In particular, the machine tool division considers that its good service and customer support has increased the level of acceptance of Polish machine tools in the British market.

Access to British expertise

The company has found it valuable to supplement its Polish technical know-how by the expertise of British salesmen and accountants. In general, the sales activities are jointly shared by British and Polish personnel, with administration, distribution, and finance being carried out by British personnel.

Access to British expertise was considered to be important at the starting-up phase, particularly for the machine tool division in 1976, and it is considered that a correct blend has now been achieved between British sales expertise and Polish technical back up. Furthermore, the advice and know-how of British personnel on packaging and presentation were considered to be crucial in the successful selling of small tools.

Case study no.3: Skorimpex Rind Limited

(i) Company background

Skorimpex Rind Limited was established in 1976, when the Polish foreign trade organization Skorimpex purchased the company Rind Utility, a London-based importer and exporter of leather goods. The new company was financed by a loan from Skorimpex, but this loan has now been repaid and the company operates as an independent British firm. The previous owner was retained as an adviser until his death, and an ex-employee of the previous company who was formerly engaged in design and selling has established his own company, Shuimpex (Services) Limited, to continue these activities from Skorimpex Rind's offices.

Rind Utility previously held an exclusive import distribution. for Polish-made shoes, distributing these products on its own account throughout the UK market. It commenced this activity in the early 1960s following an initial UK visit of a trade delegation from Skorimpex in 1960, with an exclusive agency being granted later as sales turnover increased satisfactorily. When the owner of Rind Utility decided in 1974 to sell his company as a result of his advancing years, Skorimpex was offered first option, which it accepted and concluded in 1976. The company currently employs twenty-one people including those employed by Shuimpex. Of these, five are Polish nationals employed at senior executive levels.

(ii) Company activities

The company's main activity consists of the import of Polish-made shoes and other leather products into the United Kingdom. Leather shoes predominate in this product mix, accounting at the time of interview for some £12m as compared with less than £½m for fur and leather jackets. In addition, the company has set up a subsidiary, Rind International Limited, to import shoes made from polymer materials from manufacturers in the Far East, in order to offer a complete product range. This is considered to be particularly important in the present British market, which has changed rapidly since 1978 to a position where around 50 per cent of sales are accounted for by cheaper shoes having uppers made from synthetic materials. Since Polish producers have concentrated on the manufacture of leather shoes, it is necessary for the company to extend its product range from Far Eastern sources.

Since 1978 the company has also been engaged in the export of British products for use in shoe manufacture in Poland. This new activity has included the export from the United Kingdom of adhesives and sole units, to assist Skorimpex in its responsibilities of securing Polish imports of hides, compounds, dyestuffs, and chemicals as well as the export of shoes and other finished products. At the time of interview the value of British exports was between £10m and £12m per annum, with some products handled on the company's own account and others on a commission basis. In addition, the company is frequently engaged in the purchase of spare parts for production machinery and other equipment in the Polish shoe industry. The company also provides a claims handling service for items returned under customers' complaints, but the level of returns is considered to be small as a consequence of the practice of providing samples of new goods for buyers, and the operation of an inspection system in Poland.

Finally, the company also uses its location in the United Kingdom to carry out financial operations on behalf of its parent foreign trade organization in Poland. An example of such an operation is the payment made to an Australian exporter for some hides provided to Skorimpex, Poland.

The company is engaged in the normal transport insurance activities associated with the export and import of goods, and generally uses forwarding agents for shipping activities. It usually receives goods by container ship from Poland, although it may use truck transport for delivery to Poland.

(iii)   Advantages and disadvantages of ownership of a British company

Income, costs, and profits
The company found it difficult to say with confidence whether the volume of sales had increased as a consequence of operating as a company instead of selling through an agency. Skorimpex had found

the previous agency agreement to be perfectly satisfactory in terms of the volume of Polish shoes being sold to the British market, commencing from a zero level in the 1960s to over 3 million pairs by 1974. Furthermore, the volume of sales in the market was influenced by so many other factors, such as weather and disposable income, that it was difficult to pinpoint exactly the degree to which a different business organization had influenced the level of sales income. In spite of these reservations, however, it would be surprising if some of the marketing advantages referred to in the following section had not led to increased turnover, particularly as the company is interested in further development of its business operations. On the other hand, it is clear that operating costs are higher when compared with selling through an agency, in view of the necessity of maintaining office accommodation and meeting the costs of employment.

Control of marketing
The company considered its physical location in the United Kingdom to be of crucial importance to its servicing of the British market, which is one of the largest Western markets for Polish shoes. In the first place it can maintain better control over pricing in view of its frequent contact with customers and the facility with which it can observe the effect of price changes on sales volume. Skorimpex had some influence over pricing previously, through participation in discussions with customers and biannual meetings with the directors of Rind Utility, but the present organizational arrangements mean that price changes can be carried out more quickly due to more frequent discussions with Skorimpex Rind Limited.

Secondly, various aspects of selling have improved as a consequence of the establishment of the company in the United Kingdom. The actual selling operation is the same as previously, using the same personnel, but the company can now make decisions and take action on its own account over such things as pricing, stockholding, and replacement of claims, without continual reference to the parent foreign trade organization in Poland. This capability leads to more customer confidence.

The company distributes 70 per cent of its sales through the large multiple retail chains, with 40 per cent of its sales through one retail chain alone. The remainder of the company's sales are distributed through wholesalers. Distribution through retail chains suits the company's style of operation very well, since the large orders obtained from these chains (usually a minimum of 5,000 pairs) are economic to produce in the six Polish factories with whom the company deals. These factories usually produce between 5 and 10 million pairs of shoes annually. Distribution is further improved through the ability of the company to hold stock in warehouse accommodation. This is sometimes necessary because a customer may not be able to accept an order at a particular time because of market fluctuations or lack of storage facilities.

Most of the company's promotional activity is carried out through exhibitions. These include a large national exhibition held annually in London and Blackpool at which the company hires a hotel and showroom accommodation for its own use, and exhibitions held two to three times each year at a large hotel in Leicester, near to its largest customer. The company finds it easier to organize this promotional activity, since the arrangements can all be handled on the company's own account.

The company has found that all aspects of marketing Polish products in the United Kingdom are now better as a consequence of its closeness to the market, which provides the opportunity to obtain far more timely and relevant information. Furthermore, decision making is much faster, and this benefits customer relations.

Financial and legal aspects
The company has not found it necessary to attempt to obtain any British equity capital, and has selected the limited company format as this is the usual form of business operation in the United Kingdom. Although the company has access to borrowing facilities through its own British bank it has not made use of them, preferring to finance operations from its own income.

Case study no.4: FLT and Metals Company Limited

(i)   Company background

The company was first established in 1974 by its owners Impexmetal (83 per cent shareholding), Anglo-Dal (16.7 per cent shareholding), and Dal (0.3 per cent). A company office is maintained in the City of London, and an office and warehouse in London, chiefly for the distribution of bearings. The level of turnover was over £63m in 1981, and the company currently employs some twenty people, including seven Polish nationals who hold executive positions.

(ii) Company activities

The company is engaged primarily in the export of non-ferrous metal raw materials from Poland to all destinations but chiefly to Western Europe, and the export of non-ferrous metal semi-fabricates to Poland. This activity accounted for more than £61m of turnover in 1981. In addition, the company imports Polish bearings into the United Kingdom, yielding a turnover of just over £1m per annum. The company also offers the normal claims replacement offer/sales service for bearings. Freight-related insurance activities are normally arranged through brokers, and the company engages in the normal financial activities associated with metal trading.

(iii) Advantages and disadvantages of ownership of a British company

Income, costs, and profits
The company's major objective is to promote the sale of non-ferrous metals exported by its parent foreign trade organization. To achieve this, it is important to be flexible in pricing and to be able to react quickly with price changes to movements in commodity markets. This is far better achieved by being based in a Western market than attempting to carry out this activity from Warsaw. Location in London also provides the opportunity for ease of contact with the major international metal traders, better market information, and access to the Metal Exchange, leading to rapid transactions at the operating market prices. These advantages are crucial in the international trading of metals.

As a result of these advantages from location, the company considers that the income from the sales of Polish products has increased and that profits from these sales should also have been higher in spite of the costs incurred in running the company.

Control of marketing
For trade in non-ferrous metals, the company did not consider that location in the West provided it with any more marketing advantages than the locational and pricing benefits already referred to. For the selling of bearings, however, it was considered important to maintain adequate stocks to cushion the effects of some increases in delivery times from Poland and to maintain customer confidence that adequate supplies were available for distribution.

Financial and legal aspects

The company has not found it necessary to approach British financial institutions for equity capital. Furthermore, the company has only used British credit facilities in one instance, to finance exports of non-ferrous metal semi-fabricates, worth approximately £½m to Poland. The company also uses British banks for carrying out financial transfers, but generally finds the Polish Bank Handlowy to be cheaper. The company operates as a limited company, since this is the normal type of business operation in the United Kingdom.

Better acceptance in the market

The company considers that its reliability, and its capability to carry out every stage of a business deal, has promoted better acceptance in the market for Polish products.

Access to British business expertise

The company considers it to be useful to use the expertise of its British staff in the various support and administrative functions, but views its access to the circle of metal dealers located in the City of London as absolutely crucial to its operations.

Case study no.5: Ridpath Pek Limited

(i)   Company background

Ridpath Pek Limited is a jointly-owned Anglo-Polish company engaged in the distribution of Polish meat products in the British market. The Polish ownership of the company is partly through Animex, the foreign trade organization responsible for the import and export of animal products, and partly through Anglo-Dal, a British-registered company owned by the Polish foreign trade organization Dal. The British owners are Ridpath Brothers (UK) Limited. The trade name 'Pek' has been used for many years in the British market, for a range of Polish exported preservatives.

Dal was originally established as a private Polish company prior to the Second World War, to distribute Polish meat products in export markets. Before the establishment of this company each Polish meat producer and canner had distributed its own products, but the formation of Dal led to economies of scale in marketing and distribution, and production to uniform quality. This latter task was achieved by working to specifications developed by the Polish

Central Institute of Standardization (CIS) at the request of Dal. Since the functions of marketing and distribution were now handled by Dal, the individual meat producers and canners were free to concentrate on consistent production.

Following partial nationalization of the meat industry and state control of foreign trade activities after the Second World War, the export of most meat products was the responsibility of the Animex foreign trade organization, whilst Anglo-Dal became Animex's sole representative in the UK market, distributing Polish food and by-products through a series of British importers. At approximately the same time, Anglo-Dal was expanding its representative activities into a range of other products including metals and coffee, and a decision was subsequently made to create several specialized departments to handle particular parts of the broad product range. The task of representing meat and bacon products was passed to the Animex department of Anglo-Dal, which sold its products through a series of some thirteen agents and employed, amongst others, a representative of the Polish CIS to act as a quality inspector.

In order to obtain a more unified marketing and pricing policy, the Animex department of Anglo-Dal decided to move from its position of representative to that of a centralized and specialized marketing company. Consequently, it was decided to form a joint company with one of the previous importers, Ridpath Brothers. This arrangement was also considered to be advantageous to the British partners in view of the rights of exclusive distributorship which were an intrinsic part of the business arrangement, and the closer involvement of the Polish partner in the selling operation.

(ii) Company activities

At the time of interview the company's annual turnover amounted to some £26m, the bulk of which is earned from the sale of Polish meat products to the British market. In addition, meat products are now being sourced from other areas within the EEC and sold under the Pek label with a view to broadening the supply base and increasing turnover. The company also acts as buyers for relevant Polish food requirements when these occur. Apart from these selling activities, the company is responsible for complete marketing and after-sales activities. Marketing information and predictions, including required changes in the product mix and the expected effects of new regulations, are transmitted to Poland to assist exporters and producers in their plans.

The company has also been engaged in meat slicing and packing activities, but these operations have now been curtailed as some inconsistency in supplies adversely influenced the economic utilization of the plant. Consequently, part of the relevant machinery was returned to Poland where operating costs were slightly cheaper and where further economic advantages were gained by locating cutting and packing operations closer to the source of supply, thereby avoiding weight loss in transit.

(iii)   *Advantages and disadvantages of ownership of a British company*

Income, costs, and profits
The company considers that part-ownership leads to a higher level of sales and higher income from sales in the United Kingdom than if other methods of distribution (such as sales through an agency) were used. The operating costs are also higher because of involvement in a broader range of activities, but not too high to prevent profits from also being higher than sales through an agency. These economic benefits were not regarded as the prime reason for the establishment of the company, when compared with the better potential for control over marketing and closer liaison between all sides of the industry.

Control of marketing
The company considers that all elements of marketing Polish meat products in the United Kingdom are better as a consequence of ownership as compared to representation. A unified pricing policy has been considered to be particularly important, together with advertising campaigns to promote the Polish brand name. Distribution and market information are also generally considered to be better, and decision making is faster.

Financial and legal aspects
The limited liability corporate status was selected for business operations in view of it being the normal vehicle for such operations in the United Kingdom. It gave a framework for providing British and Polish equity capital for the operation and was also a means of attracting funds from British and Polish sources of borrowing.

Acceptance in the market
The company is of the view that Polish meat products had been

readily accepted in the British market prior to the company's establishment. This market acceptance has continued and grown.

Access to British business expertise
The Polish owners of the company believe that access to competent and reliable business partners has been a crucial factor in the operation of the business. From the other side, the British partners view Polish investment in the company as an indication of the long-term commitment of their Polish partners to the British market.

Conclusions from the case studies

The structured interviews with executives from a sample of British affiliates of socialist multinationals have provided the following information on the managerial policies and practices of these companies.

Company activities

(i) The main activities of the majority of companies interviewed in this sample consisted of the import into the United Kingdom of products made in the country of origin of the socialist owners. The one exception to this general rule was FLT and Metals Company Limited, which was primarily engaged in general world-wide export trading activities related to Polish products, using London as a location for reasons of access to the Metal Exchange.

(ii) In addition, the majority of the companies were also engaged in export activities related to exports to the socialist country in which the parent foreign trade organization was domiciled. The companies consequently played important roles in the sourcing of relevant imports for the socialist owners, and they also assisted Western companies in their export activities.

(iii) Each of these import and export activities were sometimes supplemented by exporting and importing from and to other locations besides the socialist country of ownership and the United Kingdom. As mentioned previously, this was a major activity of FLT and Metals Company anyway, but other companies sometimes found it necessary to source from third countries to broaden their product range (for example synthetic material shoes from the Far East), and they also found it useful to use the UK company as a base for re-export to other markets.

(iv) All of the companies engaged in the sale of manufactured products also provided a complete after-sales service.

(v) No company carried out product and process licensing activities within the United Kingdom, although one company (Toolmex Polmach) was engaged in the setting up of industrial cooperation agreements between Polish organizations and British companies, and acted as agent for Polservice.

(vi) None of the sample companies were engaged in manufacturing activities, with the exception of some meat slicing and packaging carried out by Ridpath Pek Limited. This is hardly surprising in view of the lower direct costs of production in Eastern Europe compared with the United Kingdom, the apparent lack of many market niches in which the socialist countries might have a technological advantage, and the predominantly 'trading' profile of the foreign trade organizations engaged in company ownership.

(vii) The only insurance, freight, shipping, and financial activities carried out by the sample companies were the normal tasks related to their import and export activities.

Advantages and disadvantages of company ownership

(i) The sample companies were divided in their views concerning whether company ownership led to higher sales, income, and profits as compared with operating from Eastern Europe through an agency. All of the companies agreed that costs were certainly higher because of the expenditure necessary to set up a company, acquire premises, and employ permanent staff. In most recent cases, it was expected that improved marketing would provide sales income in excess of those costs, but economic problems in the West in general, and in the United Kingdom in particular, had prevented the generation of high sales incomes.

(ii) In spite of these problems, none of the companies stated that income and profits were lower than operating through other modes of selling and distribution. It thus appears that these companies are:

— providing their owners with much-needed foreign currency;
— covering their costs of operation, and also generating some profits as a basis for future investment;
— looking towards improved trading conditions to create the environment for better business performance.

(iii) All of the companies were strongly of the opinion that their presence in the West enabled them to market their socialist-manufactured products far better than selling through agents. The reasons for this improved marketing were as follows:

— a close physical location to the market, with associated improved access to sources of market information;
— the possibility of pricing products much nearer to the relevant 'market price', together with the possibility of achieving unified pricing (for example unified meat product pricing by Ridpath Pek Limited);
— the possibility of arriving at a product range much closer to the requirements of the market, as a result of better market information;
— the possibility of focusing promotional material much more closely to the requirements of the market;
— faster decision making because of close proximity to the market;
— finally, and of major importance for manufactured products and capital equipment, the opportunity to provide a far better after-sales service.

(iv) Most of the companies found access to British expertise to be important in the establishment and day-to-day running of the company. This British expertise was usually joined in a beneficial fashion to detailed product knowledge provided by the socialist owners.

Soviet and Eastern European investment in the Republic of Ireland

Research in this area has revealed the presence of only two Irish affiliates of socialist multinationals, namely Tungsram Manufacturers (Ireland) Limited and Gaelpirin Teoranta, which are both listed in the 1983 Carleton *Directory*. Letters to the Professor of Marketing of the National Institute for Higher Education, Limerick, the Confederation of Irish Industry, Dublin, and the Department of Industry and Energy, Dublin, although confirming the existence of Tungsram Manufacturers (Ireland) did not yield the names of other companies.

This small number of companies compared with those in the United Kingdom can be partly explained by the small size of the Irish market and by the comparative ease with which this market can be served by companies located in the United Kingdom itself. What made these Irish-registered companies different, however, was that they were both either intended, or operational, manufacturing concerns. Tungsram Manufacturers (Ireland) was a joint Hungarian/ Western company (with the majority of shares owned by the Hungarian side) established in Cork for the manufacture of light bulbs, whilst Gaelpirin Teoranta was intending to set itself up as a joint Bulgarian/Western operation to manufacture leather clothing in the West of Ireland. At the time of carrying out this research the Irish state-supported grant-aided operating industrial development body (Udaras na Gaeltachta) was awaiting approval for this venture from the Irish government.[12]

In view of the probable uniqueness of Ireland as a Western European country acting as host to an Eastern European manufacturing concern, it was decided to study the Tungsram operation in more detail. An interview was obtained in the spring of 1983 with a director of the British distributors of products made at the Irish factory. The information obtained from this interview is presented in the following pages, followed by a summary of information on the subsequent closure of the factory in 1984.

Case study: Tungsram Manufacturers (Ireland) Limited[13]

(i)   Company background

Tungsram (Ireland) Limited was established in Little Island, County Cork during November 1980 for the manufacture of electric light bulbs. The factory was some 55,000 square feet in area, and the buildings and equipment represent an investment of some £4.5m.[14] The production capacity came on stream in April 1982, commencing deliveries to the United Kingdom in May of that year. It was intended that the production capacity of the three lines of machines would be assimilated by the end of 1983, to achieve an annual output of 20 million bulbs per annum. At the time of interview the available factory area was approximately one-third occupied and further developments were envisaged, such as diversification into a broader product range or an expansion in output of the B-22 range of lamps, which had market potential in the United Kingdom, Commonwealth countries, France, and Belgium.

(ii) Company ownership

The major shareholders in the factory were the United Incandescent Lamp and Electrical Company Limited (Budapest) (i.e. Tungsram) and the Hungarian Foreign Trade Bank, with shares also held by J.J. Bustin & Company of London and Terra Nova of Ireland.

Tungsram (Hungary)

Tungsram is a Hungarian-based multinational group concerned with the development, production, and distribution of electrical lighting products together with the equipment required for their manufacture. At the time of interview it was the sixth largest manufacturer of lighting equipment in the world, behind G.E., Westinghouse, Sylvania, Philips, and Osram. In 1983 the organization employed 36,000 people in seventeen factories located in Hungary. It is also engaged in the export and import of lighting products and associated manufacturing machinery.[15] As an extension of its foreign trade activities in manufacturing equipment, Tungsram is engaged in the provision of turnkey factories and has provided sets of manufacturing equipment to enterprises in more than twenty-five countries.[16] As a consequence of its range and volume of foreign trade activities, Tungsram is now reputed to be the largest single earner of foreign currency in Hungary.

Of more recent interest, however, has been Tungsram's investment activities in Western manufacturing companies as a means to service its international customers from the most appropriate source of supply, bearing in mind manufacturing and transport costs, prices, and currency exchange rates. To date, Tungsram has invested in four such companies, namely Action-Tungsram in the United States, the Aslo Electric Company in Pakistan, Tungsram (Ireland) Limited,[17] and a factory in Vienna.

According to a recent report,[18] Tungsram held 64 per cent of the share capital ($1m)[19] in Tungsram (Ireland) Limited, and the organization also provided equipment and production machinery worth some $3.8m. This machinery was installed by Hungarian technicians, who subsequently trained the Irish labour force, and Tungsram also maintained a technical management role. Following the American and Pakistani operations, Tungsram (Ireland) Limited was the Hungarian company's third joint venture since 1978 but the first where the Hungarian company had more than 50 per cent of the shareholding.[20] A further 12 per cent of the capital was provided by the Hungarian Foreign Trade Bank, and this would appear to have been one of the first cases of the Bank's recent activities in Western joint ventures.[21]

J.J. Bustin & Company Limited

This London-based company is the representative and agent in the British market for Tungsram. It has been operating in the United Kingdom for the past twelve to thirteen years, and distribute and markets a wide range of Hungarian lighting products. These include a range of different types of light bulbs, and control components. One of the main activities of the company is the distribution and marketing of Hungarian-made automobile light bulbs. The company began sourcing B-22 lamps from Tungsram (Ireland) Limited in May 1982. It imported some 2.2 million lamps in total during July, August, and September of 1982, and intended to source 10 million lamps annually.

(iii) Company technology

The technology used by Tungsram (Ireland) Limited was completely Hungarian, using bulb assembly machines supplied by the Hungarian parent company. There was no component manufacture as such, although it was sometimes necessary to carry out certain modification processes to purchased components before they were ready for assembly. The products from the factory met all of the British Standards requirements for light output, service life, and safety, and Economic Commission for Europe (ECE) requirements for quality control during manufacture.

(iv) Component supplies

Seventy per cent of all the individual components used in the assembly of light bulbs in Tungsram (Ireland) Limited were sourced from British or other EEC suppliers. The gas was purchased from the Irish subsidiary of BOC, and the packaging was all Irish-made and printed. The components imported from Hungary were the filament and the cement.

(v) Company location

Prior to the selection of Cork as the site for the company, Tungsram surveyed a number of other sites in France, Italy, the United

Kingdom, and Ireland. The Cork site was finally selected because of the financial incentives to overseas investors in Ireland and the availability of supplies of natural gas.

(vi) Company closure

The company subsequently ceased operations in February 1984 for reasons of overcapacity and supply difficulties, according to a report in the *Financial Times*.[22] Indeed that same report quoted a member of the Tungsram Budapest management as describing the Irish venture as 'having been virtually doomed from the start'. The management at Tungsram's Budapest headquarters also underwent some change immediately prior to the closure, and apparently followed a policy of retrenchment after a financial loss in 1982. A further *Financial Times* report[23] also refers to the Hungarian management taking steps to rectify a policy of over-ambitious growth in total production capacity during the 1970s, bearing in mind the actual market demand during the 1980s, particularly in the United Kingdom.

An executive of the company's British shareholders expressed a view to the author in June 1984 that the company had been gaining low returns on investment as a consequence of a downturn in market demand giving rise to excess capacity in the industry and minimal profit margins on sales. Running costs in general, and fuel costs in particular, were also found to be comparatively high, and since the company had not had sufficient time to diversify into high-margin products it was obliged to cease trading to prevent low returns on investment. It is clear therefore that subsidiaries of Soviet and Eastern European multinationals face financial challenges caused by markets and production costs similar to those of their Western counterparts, and the experience of Tungsram (Ireland) Limited reinforces the case for further substantial research on Soviet and Eastern European investment in Western countries.

Conclusions and suggestions for further research

This preliminary research on British subsidiaries of Soviet and Eastern European multinationals has yielded much useful information on the scope and scale of the activities of these organizations. Furthermore, the information obtained from the other IRM-commissioned studies of the activities of these organizations in

Austria, Germany, and Sweden presented elsewhere in this volume in no way contradicts the results of the research presented in this chapter, from which it is possible to draw the following conclusions.

(i)   The overwhelming majority of the subsidiaries of Soviet and Eastern European multinationals were engaged in service activities. Of these, the great majority were engaged in marketing-related service activities to promote the sale in Western markets of products manufactured in the respective socialist country. In addition, many of these companies also acted as purchasing agents for a defined range of supplies required by their domestic industry. It would be useful, therefore, to continue further research on these subsidiaries to determine their overall effectiveness as marketing and distribution channels in East–West trade.

(ii)   Several of the subsidiaries of Soviet and Eastern European foreign trade organizations were found to be engaged in the service activities of transport, insurance, and banking. Furthermore, many of these companies appeared to be performing quite well in terms of the normal Western criteria used to judge company performance. It is probable that these activities may continue to grow in Western countries, and they should continue to be monitored in line with other studies of multinational service operations. It is unlikely that they will grow from a basis of technological advantage, however, although one subsidiary has recently been approved for calibration purposes by the British Calibration Service.[24]

(iii)   The majority of the subsidiaries of Soviet and Eastern European foreign trade organizations were established in the 1960s and 1970s when East–West trade was expanding rapidly. Although the number of these companies will probably continue to grow, it is unlikely that it will grow as rapidly as in those two decades, unless East–West trade grows at a much faster rate than at present.

(iv)   The number of these subsidiaries is comparatively small when compared with the number of Western multinationals, but the number of Soviet and Eastern European organizations having the legal competence to invest overseas is also comparatively small. On the other hand, it was found that more than 50 per cent of foreign trade organizations in some of the socialist countries were engaged in multinational activities in Western countries. Consequently, the number of companies is probably restricted not by the propensity to invest by foreign trade organizations but by the availability of scarce Western currency for investment.

(v)   The scale of operation of Soviet and Eastern European

subsidiaries was found to be very small in terms of total turnover and investment. To a very great extent, this is a reflection of the comparatively small volume of East–West trade and the scarcity of Western currency. It can be concluded from this, therefore, that Western governments need not be over-concerned about the possible influence of these subsidiary companies on national economic activities in the host country. Any national policies directed towards these companies, therefore, will probably be a reflection of trade and foreign affairs policies towards the country of their parent organizations.

(vi)   It is considered that further useful work could be carried out on longitudinal studies of the development of these companies, updating much of the information presented in this chapter. Furthermore, increased efforts could be made to secure interviews with a wider range of companies and to monitor such companies to establish whether their business performance is closely influenced by general trading conditions.

(vii)   The parent Soviet and Eastern European multinationals (or foreign trade organizations) are themselves worthy of further study from the viewpoint of their international objectives and strategies as related to investment in Western countries. Particular attention should also be paid to their activities in developing countries, where they may well have certain technological and pricing advantages compared with host companies and Western multinational enterprises. Dal and Metalexport of Poland, Tungsram of Hungary, and Soyuzneftexport of the Soviet Union would appear to be good subjects for the commencement of such a study in view of the scale of their activities in Western markets.

Notes and references

1. See D.E. Franklin, 'Exporting to Eastern Europe: Principles and Practice', unpublished doctoral thesis, University of Aston in Birmingham, 1981. Some of the results of Franklin's research have recently been published as 'Dealing with East European Importing Organizations: A Survey of UK Exporters' Experience', *European Journal of Marketing*, **16**, No.7 (1982).
2. See, for example, H.E. Meyer, 'This Communist Internationale Has a Capitalist Accent', *Fortune*, February 1977, pp. 134–48; C.H. McMillan, 'Growth of External Investments by the Comecon Countries', *The World Economy*, **2**, No.3 (September 1979), pp. 363–86; P. Hill, 'Les proies des multis rouges', *Vision*, February 1977, pp. 44–8; M.I. Goldman, *The*

Enigma of Soviet Petroleum: Half Full or Half Empty?, London, George Allen & Unwin, 1980, pp. 72–87.
3. See G. Hamilton, Introduction and Conclusion to this book.
4. These values of average export turnovers were calculated by dividing the export sales for each country as presented in the *1979 Yearbook of International Trade Statistics* (UN, New York) and the *Yearbook of the Member Countries of the Council for Mutual Economic Assistance*, by the number of foreign trade organizations for each country listed in *Trade Contacts in Eastern Europe* (London Chamber of Commerce and Industry, 1980).
5. The proportion of export sales delivered to the developed market economies during the late 1970s was as follows: Bulgaria 11 per cent, Czechoslovakia 21 per cent, GDR 20 per cent, Hungary 44 per cent, Poland 33 per cent, Romania 35 per cent, Soviet Union 29 per cent (calculated from data provided in the sources cited in n.4).
6. B. Morgan (ed.), *Directory of Soviet and East European Companies in the West*, Ottawa, Institute of Soviet and East European Studies, Carleton University, 1979.
7. Ibid.
8. See C.H. McMillan, *Direct Soviet and East European Investment in the Industrialized Western Economies*, Working Paper No.7, East–West Commercial Relations Series, Institute of Soviet and East European Studies, Carleton University, Ottawa, 1978, p. 13.
9. See Central Statistical Office, *United Kingdom Balance of Payments 1982 Edition*, HMSO, Table 11.2. A figure of £13,855m is given for the direct net assets of overseas companies in the UK private sector in 1979, and a total of £26,480m, including oil companies' investments and net borrowing from banks during that same year. For 1980, the respective figures are £16,315m and £29,565m.
10. See *Banker's Almanac*, 1980–81, IPC, London, 1981.
11. Goldman (1980), pp. 72–6.
12. *Private Communications (Udaras na Gaeltachta)*, 4 November 1982 and 2 March 1983.
13. The majority of the data for this case study was obtained from an interview with Mr P. Bustin, Director of J.J. Bustin & Company, and also Director of Tungsram Manufacturers (Ireland) Limited. Other sources of numerical data are cited separately.
14. *ESB Prospect*, August 1982, pp. 8–9.
15. See n.2, and the Hungarian journal *New Hungarian Exporter*, 32, No.3 (March 1982), pp. 12–13, for a description of investment in Tungsram's Hungarian plants.
16. *New Hungarian Exporter*, 32, No.11 (November 1982), p. 21. This report cites the establishment of light production plants using Tungsram components, machinery, and technology in Zaire, Ghana, and Kenya.
17. *New Hungarian Exporter*, 52, No.7/8 (July/August 1982), p. 26. As well as referring to the American, Pakistani, and Irish operations, this report cites the establishment in the late 1960s of factories using Tungsram equipment in India, Syria, Thailand, Iran, Iraq, Ghana, Indonesia, and Morocco.

18. See n.17.
19. See the 1983 Carleton *Directory* (C.H. McMillan and P. Egyed (eds),
    *East–West Business Directory: A Listing of Companies in the West with Soviet
    and East European Equity Participation*, London, Duncan Publishing,
    1983).
20. See n.17.
21. See n.17, and *New Hungarian Exporter*, **32**, No.12 (December 1982), p. 9.
22. 'Hungarians to close Irish light bulb plant', *Financial Times*, 2 February
    1984.
23. 'Tungsram tempers expansion aims', *Financial Times*, 14 February
    1984.
24. CZ Scientific Instruments Limited have received approval from the
    British Calibration Service for their laboratories to be used for
    calibration of measuring instruments and machines. See British
    Calibration Service, *Approved Laboratories and Their Measurement*,
    September 1984, p. 25.

3 Soviet and Eastern European company activity in Sweden

Malcolm R. Hill

Number of companies

In this chapter a selection of Swedish-registered companies owned or partially owned by Soviet and Eastern European foreign trade organizations is examined in a similar manner to the British sample in the preceding chapter.[1] It was decided to select Sweden as a country for study in this present research, as company reporting regulations in operation in that country are similar to those in the United Kingdom. An original list of twenty-eight companies was compiled primarily from the prepublication issue of the Carleton *Directory*[2] and supplemented by information from the Sveriges Riksbank in Stockholm.[3] This list is shown in Table 3.1 but complete comparative financial information is not available for all of the companies for the following reasons.

(a) The names provided by the Sveriges Riksbank were those of companies that had applied for a permit to receive Soviet or Eastern European investment. This permit may not have been actually used, however, since no evidence of the existence of VEB Deutrans Internationale Spedition AB, Foto Svea AB, Folke Edquist AB, Bulmak Sverige AB, or BarCol-Air AB could be found in the information provided by the Swedish Company Registry. It also transpired that Nilstal AB and Nils Ake Nilsson AB were different names for the same company, Nilstal Nils Ake Nilsson AB.

(b) In order to provide a consistent base for comparison with the British companies, the years 1979 and 1980 were cited for examination. A further five companies were thereby removed from the sample, since at the time of carrying out the research no accounts for 1979 or 1980 were available for AK Optik Instrument AB, Junemaskiner Mats Hultgren AB (last accounts 1977), and

Table 3.1 *Listing of Swedish-registered companies owned by Soviet and Eastern European foreign trade organizations*

	From Carleton *Directory* (1983)	From Sveriges Riksbank (1982)
Bulgaria		Nordcar Truck AB Bulmak Sverige AB
Czechoslovakia	Scansigma AB* Chemapol Svenska AB* Tjecho Svea AB*	Zetor Sweden AB
GDR	AK Optik Instrument AB	Foto Svea AB Gunnar B. Janson AB Svenska Wemex AB VEB Deutrans Inter- nationale Spedition AB Soemtronic AB Folke Edquist AB
Hungary	Tungsram AB* Bygging-Ungern 31 AB*	

Poland	Nordiska Unipol AB*
	Nilstal AB*
	Polbatica (Svensk-Polska
	  Befraktnings) AB*
	Norbis Travel AB*
	Transryb AB*
		BarCol-Air AB
		Pol-Line AB
		Terminal-Syd AB
		Junemaskiner Mats
		  Hultgren AB
		Nils Ake Nilsson AB

Soviet Union	Matreco Handels AB* Scarus Marine Nutrition AB* Scansov Transport AB*	

* Also mentioned by the Sveriges Riksbank.

Pol-Line AB (last accounts 1978). Furthermore, Soemtronic AB went into liquidation during 1977, and Terminal-Syd AB does not appear to have actively traded in the years specified. Transryb AB also had to be eliminated, through lack of data.

This elimination resulted in a final sample of sixteen Swedish-registered companies with socialist foreign trade organization ownership (see Tables 3.2 and 3.3). Four of these were 100 per cent owned by Soviet or Eastern European foreign trade organizations,

Table 3.2   Ownership and financial information on affiliates of socialist multinationals in Sweden, 1979*

Year established	Main business activity	Name of company	Shareholders (Eastern European)	% Eastern European ownership	Turnover	Profit before taxation	Profit after taxation	Fixed	Current	Total	Long-term	Current	Total net assets
			Ownership					Financial information (Kr)					
									Assets		Liabilities		

Bulgarian investment and ownership

| 1969 | Import/export machine parts for trucks | Nordcar Truck AB | Balkancarimpex | n.a. | | No financial data available | | | | | | | |

Czechoslovakian investment and ownership

1968	Marketing and servicing hydraulic pumps	Scansigma AB	Intersigma	n.a.	4,823,161	(4,725)		7,435	5,735,855	5,743,290	—	5,697,511	45,779
1970	Marketing chemicals and pharmaceuticals	Chemapol Svenska AB	Chemapol	50	3,736,576	228,780		40,226	2,510,131	2,550,357	—	1,928,608	621,755
1968	Marketing and servicing machine tools	Tjecho Svea AB	Strojimport	75	29,706,609	1,008,700		277,364	28,547,875	28,825,239	11,855,004	14,470,047	2,500,188
1952	Marketing and servicing vehicles	Zetor Sweden AB	Motokov	100	39,856,454	23,547		10,029,569	46,314,543	56,344,112	13,901,566	36,419,865	602,268

GDR investment and ownership

| 1957 | Marketing chemicals and metals | Gunnar B. Janson AB | Some East German interest | n.a. | 67,500,000 | 1,227,000 | | 675,000 | 22,930,000 | 23,605,000 | 11,159,000 | 9,436,000 | 3,010,000 |
| 1959 | Marketing heavy machinery | Svenska Wemex AB | Some East German interest | n.a. | 9,606,794 | 19,654 | | 1,410,404 | 9,423,968 | 10,834,372 | 960,000 | 7,902,514 | 1,971,858 |

Hungarian investment and ownership

1928	Marketing and manufacturing lamps	Tungsram AB	Tungsram	100	30,789,769	(158,705)	1,548,000	21,087,000	22,635,000	3,531,000	15,184,000	3,920,000
1969	Marketing and manufacturing construction equipment	Bygging-Ungern 31 AB	State Bldg. Enterprise No. 31	50	33,000	10,000	4,000	59,000	63,000		21,000	42,000

Polish investment and ownership

1969	Marketing wood products	Nordiska Unipol AB	Ciech, Dal, Paged	n.a.	2,940,571	404,703	181,188	2,427,133	2,608,321		2,385,134	223,187
1966	Marketing and import/export of metal products	Nilstal Nils Ake Nilsson AB	Stalexport	n.a.	8,104,232	7,642	44,500	4,058,983	4,103,483		3,996,241	107,242
1947	Transport services	Polbaltica (Svensk-Polska Befraktnings) AB	Polfracht	n.a.	1,321,436	24,178	86,700	627,606	714,306		501,405	212,901
1974	Travel agents	Norbis Travel AB	Orbis	100	9,670,081	64,365	180,302	1,121,016	1,301,318		1,136,696	164,622

Soviet investment and ownership

1957	Marketing and servicing vehicles	Matreco Handels AB	Avtoexport, Konela	100	100,210,000	1,919,000	41,476,000	82,788,000	124,264,000	65,355,000	47,419,000	11,490,000
1979	Servicing fishing fleet	Scarus Marine Nutrition AB	Sovrybflot	n.a.	617,752	31,776	89,880	385,307	475,187		261,609	213,578
1959	Transport services	Scansov Transport AB	Sovfracht	60	73,692,882	1,398,510	1,712,873	23,337,781	25,050,654		23,205,074	1,845,580

* The use of brackets denotes a negative value.
Source: Company registrations and accounts filed in the Swedish Company Registry.

Table 3.3 Ownership and financial information on affiliates of socialist multinationals in Sweden, 1980*

Year established	Main business activity	Name of company	Shareholders (Eastern European)	% Eastern European ownership	Turnover	Profit before taxation	Profit after taxation	Assets Fixed	Assets Current	Assets Total	Liabilities Long-term	Liabilities Current	Total net assets
Bulgarian investment and ownership													
1969	Import/export machine parts for trucks	Nordcar Truck AB	Balkancarimpex	n.a.	3,085,000	639,200			689,300	689,300		4,033,900	(3,344,600)
Czechoslovakian investment and ownership													
1968	Marketing and servicing hydraulic pumps	Scansigma AB	Intersigma	n.a.	3,385,264	(19,279)		4,700	4,959,376	4,964,076		4,911,109	52,967
1970	Marketing chemicals and pharmaceuticals	Chemapol Svenska AB	Chemapol	50	3,721,395	31,577		107,086	1,816,403	1,923,489		1,278,258	645,231
1968	Marketing and servicing machine tools	Tjecho Svea AB	Strojimport	75	30,575,270	1,007,594		376,274	33,102,466	33,478,740	10,972,829	19,000,285	3,505,626
1952	Marketing and servicing vehicles	Zetor Sweden AB	Motokov	100	44,244,131	26,934		8,657,115	39,718,824	48,375,939	21,253,746	21,098,967	6,023,226
GDR investment and ownership													
1957	Marketing chemicals and metals	Gunnar B. Janson AB	Some East German interest	n.a.	79,901,000	3,141,000		790,000	35,106,000	35,896,000	17,362,000	15,635,000	2,899,000
1959	Marketing heavy machinery	Svenska Wemex AB	Some East German interest	n.a.	12,289,265	8,483		2,269,781	13,496,142	15,765,923	900,000	13,308,330	1,557,593

Hungarian investment and ownership

Year	Activity	Swedish company	Foreign partner	%								
1928	Marketing and manufacturing lamps	Tungsram AB	Tungsram	100	33,682,673	438,741	2,034,000	24,266,000	26,300,000	3,051,000	18,891,000	435,800
1969	Marketing and manufacturing construction equipment	Bygging-Ungern 31 AB	State Bldg. Enterprise No. 31	50	610,495	390		206,452	206,452		163,890	42,562

Polish investment and ownership

Year	Activity	Swedish company	Foreign partner	%								
1969	Marketing wood products	Nordiska Unipol AB	Ciech. Dal. Paged	n.a.	7,571,545	484,570	251,265	5,534,802	5,786,168		5,384,016	402,152
1966	Marketing and import/export of metal products	Nilstal Nils Ake Nilsson AB	Stalexport	n.a.	7,494,229	103,638	112,200	4,374,978	4,487,178		4,283,097	204,081
1947	Transport services	Polbaltica (Svensk-Polska Befraktnings) AB	Polfracht	n.a.	1,399,346	15,986	152,000	486,837	638,837		422,460	216,377
1974	Travel agents	Norbis Travel AB	Orbis	100	11,022,625	37,009	262,131	1,377,018	1,639,149		1,511,537	127,612

Soviet investment and ownership

Year	Activity	Swedish company	Foreign partner	%								
1957	Marketing and servicing vehicles	Matreco Handels AB	Avtoexport, Konela	100	84,114,000	(11,552,000)	70,864,000	99,808,000	170,672,000	131,933,000	30,652,000	8,087,000
1979	Servicing fishing fleet	Scarus Marine Nutrition AB	Sovrybflot	n.a.	56,017,704	835,169	186,301	15,318,915	15,505,216		14,678,738	826,478
1959	Transport services	Scansov Transport AB	Sovfracht	60	144,431,418	2,564,198	2,641,854	22,506,602	25,148,456		20,955,231	4,193,225

* The use of brackets denotes a negative value.
Source: Company registrations and accounts filed in the Swedish Company Registry.

and four had between 50–100 per cent of such ownership. The percentages of socialist shareholdings in the remaining eight companies were unknown, and under Swedish company law it does not appear to be compulsory to state the extent of the owners' commitment in the articles of association or financial accounts. Therefore, in Swedish companies, unlike their British counterparts, the percentage of ownership for which Soviet and Eastern European foreign trade organizations are responsible is often unknown.

Company activities and history of operation

Tables 3.2 and 3.3 show that all of the companies are involved in marketing, import/export activities, or associated services. In addition, two companies, Tungsram AB and Bygging-Ungern 31 AB, are also concerned with manufacture. All of the companies, with the exception of Tungsram AB and Polbaltica (Svensk-Polska Befraktnings) AB, were established between the beginning of the 1950s and the end of the 1970s, with the majority of the companies established in the 1950s and 1960s and only a further three of the sixteen companies established in the 1970s. These figures suggest that the continued establishment of new affiliates of socialist multinationals in the late 1970s and early 1980s is less evident in Sweden than in the United Kingdom.

Features of Swedish financial data

It was originally intended, in this research project, to analyse the Swedish companies in a similar fashion to those studied in Britain. Since Swedish accounting practices differ from their British counterparts, however, certain assumptions had to be made with both sets of published accounts to achieve comparable figures.[4] Some of these differences have their roots in the differences in national company tax systems between the two countries, as described here for the years studied.

  (a) Profit before tax is a slightly misleading figure for comparison since Swedish companies' transfers to an 'anti-cyclical investment fund' are made prior to the declaration of this figure. This is a means of avoiding tax on profits which is heavily utilized by Swedish companies, despite the requirement to deposit an additional amount equal to 50 per cent of the transfer in a non interest-bearing account with the Sveriges Riksbank (i.e. the equivalent of the sum saved in tax). There are also other tax deductible allocations, including the inventory reserve and the statutory legal reserve.

Consequently, profit before tax and before profit allocations (*resultat fore bokslutchspositioner och skatt*) has been used in this present analysis although there might, in certain cases, have been some justification for taking some account of certain interest/commission movements. This figure was also preferred to 'profit after tax' as a basis for comparison, since the value of corporation tax averages 57 per cent in Sweden and is payable in the year that it is incurred. Therefore, the profit-after-tax figure cannot be used to compare the performance of British and Swedish companies as the UK percentage could have reached a maximum of 52 per cent.

(b) Fixed assets are also accounted for differently in the two countries. In Sweden depreciation on buildings varies between 2 and 5 per cent per annum depending on their expected economic life, and depreciation on machinery is based on 30 per cent per annum (plus acquisitions and minus sales) to be completely written off in the fifth year. As British law allowed 100 per cent depreciation on machinery in the first year, and 79 per cent on buildings in the first year with 4 per cent per annum thereafter,[5] some differences will inevitably occur in the figures.

(c) Another difference on the assets side of the Swedish company balance sheet is that small companies in particular tend to report the unutilized portion of their overdraft chequing account facilities as cash due from the bank on their current assets, and to enter the entire amount of the overdraft facility on the liabilities side under long-term debt. There is also some indication that a number of companies may include the compulsory deposit at the Sveriges Riksbank in their figures for current assets, thereby further changing the values of this financial parameter from those presented by their British counterparts.

Taking due note of these points, figures have been extracted from the published accounts of the Swedish affiliates of the socialist multinationals, and these are presented in Tables 3.2 and 3.3.

Table 3.4   *Turnover of Swedish affiliates of socialist multinationals, 1979 and 1980*

Country of ownership	1979 turnover (Kr)	1980 turnover (Kr)
Bulgaria	n.a.	3,085,000
Czechoslovakia	78,122,800	81,926,060
GDR	77,106,794	92,190,265
Hungary	30,822,769	34,293,168
Poland	22,036,320	27,487,745
Soviet Union	174,520,634	284,563,122
Total	382,609,317	523,545,360

Note: Exchange rates between the Swedish krona and the US dollar were 4.28 and 4.23 in 1979 and 1980 respectively, and exchange rates between the US dollar and the pound sterling were 2.122669 and 2.32577 respectively (see *UN Yearbook of International Trade Statistics*, 1980). Thus the rate of exchange between the krona and the pound was some 9.1 in 1979 and 9.80 in 1980.
Sources: Compiled from data shown in Tables 3.2 and 3.3

Company turnover

The total turnover figures for Swedish affiliates of socialist multi-nationals are provided in Table 3.4, from which it can be seen that the total turnover of these companies was some Kr380m in 1979 and some Kr520m in 1980. Consequently, turnover appeared to increase by some 36 per cent for these companies from 1979 to 1980, with increases in aggregate turnover for each of the socialist countries but especially those from the Soviet Union (Scarus Marine Nutrition AB and Scansov Transport AB).

If it is assumed that £1 was approximately equal to Kr10 during those years (see footnote to Table 3.4), it would appear that the total turnover for these companies was more than £35m in 1979 and £50m in 1980. This total turnover is far lower than that for the British affiliates of socialist multinationals during those same years even when the large turnover figure for Nafta (GB) Limited is discounted. The average turnover for a Swedish affiliate was found to be some £2–3m per annum during the years studied, whereas the average turnover for the British affiliates, even when the turnover for Nafta (GB) was discounted, was more than £10m per annum.

Using turnover as a criterion, the socialist country which is best represented in ownership of Swedish affiliates is the Soviet Union, followed by the GDR and Czechoslovakia, and then Hungary. Poland is less well established, especially when compared with the turnover of Polish companies within the United Kingdom, whilst Bulgarian activity is very small and that of Romania non-existent.

Assets

Data for the assets and liabilities of Swedish affiliates of socialist multinationals are provided in Tables 3.2 and 3.3. These show that the majority of the companies' assets are accounted for by current assets, which are almost balanced by current and long-term liabilities. This is partly to be expected from the nature of the business in which these companies are engaged and the special features of Swedish accounting practices referred to earlier.

Data for total fixed assets and net assets of Swedish affiliates of socialist multinationals are summarized in Table 3.5. It can be seen that the total fixed assets for the Swedish affiliates increased from Kr57m in 1979 to Kr88m in 1980, whilst the total net assets remained at Kr24m for both years, although this latter figure includes a negative value of Kr3m for the net assets of the Bulgarian-owned Swedish affiliate. The assets of Soviet-owned companies account for a large proportion of these total figures: more than 75 per cent of the

Table 3.5 *Total fixed assets and total net assets of Swedish affiliates of socialist multinationals, 1979 and 1980**

Country of ownership	Fixed assets (Kr)		Net assets (Kr)	
	1979	1980	1979	1980
Bulgaria	n.a.		n.a.	(3,344,600)
Czechoslovakia	10,354,594	9,145,175	3,210,410	6,491,278
GDR	2,085,404	3,059,781	3,207,185	3,054,759
Hungary	1,552,000	2,034,000	3,932,000	4,400,562
Poland	492,690	777,596	707,952	950,582
Soviet Union	43,278,753	73,692,155	13,549,158	13,106,703
Total	57,763,441	88,708,707	24,606,705	24,659,284

* The use of brackets denotes a negative value
Sources: Compiled from data shown in Tables 3.2 and 3.3.

fixed assets, and 55 per cent of the net assets. The majority of this Soviet investment, in turn, is accounted for by the assets of one company alone, namely Matreco Handels AB, a company engaged in the marketing and servicing of vehicles, which increased its fixed assets from Kr41m in 1979 to Kr70m in 1980.

Finally, it is useful to compare the investment figures for these Swedish companies with those of their British counterparts. The total fixed assets for over forty British companies in 1979 and 1980 was some £23m, giving an average of approximately £½m per company, whereas for the sixteen listed Swedish companies the total fixed assets were some £6m, and the net assets some £2.5m (see Table 3.6).

Table 3.6   *Profitability of Swedish affiliates of socialist multinationals, 1979 and 1980**

Company	Profit-before-tax†/turnover (%)		Profit-before-tax†/total assets (%)		Profit-before-tax†/net assets (%)	
	1979	1980	1979	1980	1979	1980
Nordcar Truck AB	n.a.	20.7	n.a.	92.7	n.a.	(19.1)
Scansigma AB	(0.1)	(0.6)	(0.08)	(0.4)	(10.3)	(36.4)
Chemapol Svenska AB	6.1	0.8	8.9	1.6	36.8	4.9
Tjecho Svea AB	3.4	3.3	3.5	3.0	40.3	28.7
Zetor Sweden AB	0.06	0.06	0.04	0.06	0.4	0.4
Gunnar B. Janson AB	1.8	3.9	5.2	8.7	40.8	108.3
Svenska Wemex AB	0.2	0.07	0.2	0.06	1.0	0.5
Tungsram AB	(0.5)	1.3	(0.7)	1.7	4.0	100.6
Bygging-Ungern 31 AB	30.3	0.06	15.9	0.2	23.3	0.9
Nordiska Unipol AB	13.8	6.4	15.5	8.4	181.3	120.5
Nilstal Nils Ake Nilsson AB	0.09	1.4	0.2	2.3	7.1	50.8
Polbaltica (Svensk-Polska Befraktnings) AB	1.8	1.1	3.4	2.5	11.3	7.4
Norbis Travel AB	0.7	0.4	4.9	2.3	39.1	29.0
Matreco Handels AB	1.9	(13.7)	.1 5.	(6.8)	16.7	(142.8)
Scarus Marine Nutrition AB	5.1	1.5	6.7	5.4	14.9	101.0
Scansov Transport AB	1.9	1.8	5.6	10.2	75.8	61.1

The use of brackets denotes a negative value.
† And before profit allocations.
Sources: Compiled from data shown in Tables 3.2 and 3.3

Thus, the average fixed assets for the Swedish affiliates work out at approximately £375,000, and the net assets at approximately £160,000. Consequently, the average level of investment of socialist multinationals appears to be lower in Swedish affiliates than in their British counterparts by a factor of two.

Profitability

An analysis of the profitability of Swedish affiliates of socialist multinationals is provided in Table 3.6. It is apparent from this analysis that there are wide fluctuations for these ratios between companies and also between the two consecutive years under consideration.

The author was unable to discover a Swedish equivalent of the British publication of inter-company comparisons as a backcloth against which to analyse these financial ratios. Some earlier research by Pratten[6] had suggested that Swedish firms in general performed better than their British counterparts, although there are several shortcomings in the application of Pratten's data to the present study. These include the age of Pratten's data (1973), his selection of manufacturing firms, and the use of sales, value added, investment, and export indices on a per employee basis.

Conclusions which may be drawn from this representation must, of necessity, be tentative, but the similarities in the distribution for profitability indices between the British and Swedish samples are striking. Approximately 80 per cent of UK affiliates fell below the median in profit margins analyses, as they did in the profits/total assets analyses, when compared with a large sample of UK businesses.[7] In the Swedish sample between 73–81 per cent of affiliates returned a profit margin less than the median of this index for British companies, and 86 per cent performed at a level lower than the median of British companies on the profits/total assets ratio (see Table 3.7 and Chapter 2). These profits/turnover and profits/total assets figures suggests that, as for their British counterparts, Swedish-registered companies owned by Eastern European foreign trade organizations are less profitable than wholly Western-owned companies. Consequently, it is likely that these companies are primarily viewed by their owners as avenues to secure Western currency, with sufficient profits being generated to remain in business and generate some expansion.

The profit/net assets ratios are not very reliable for assessing the

Table 3.7   *Ranges of profitability of Swedish affiliates of socialist multinationals, 1979 and 1980*

(A) Profit margin				
1979				
Spread (%)	< 0.7	0.7–5.0	5.0–15.9	> 15.9
No. of companies	6	5	3	1
1980				
Spread (%)	< 0.8	0.8–5.1	5.1–12.1	> 12.1
No. of companies	6	7	1	2
(b) Profit/total assets				
1979				
Spread (%)	< 3.0	3.0–8.9	8.9–20.6	> 20.6
No. of companies	6	7	2	0
1980				
Spread (%)	< 2.3	2.3–10.3	10.3–19.5	> 19.5
No. of companies	7	7	0	2
(c) Rate of capital employed				
1979				
Spread (%)	< 7.7	7.7–17.4	17.4–48.7	> 48.7
No. of companies	4	3	4	4
1980				
Spread (%)	< 4.2	4.2–19.9	19.9–54.9	> 54.9
No. of companies	6	2	3	5

Source: Compiled from data shown in Table 3.6

business performance of these companies since liabilities do not consistently include loans from the parent companies, and the results are extremely varied, as they are also for the sample of British companies discussed in the previous chapter. High ratios of profit/net assets are attributed to small net assets as companies tend to match assets and liabilities, thereby producing a high margin on capital employed.

Comments, conclusions, and suggestions for further research

(i)   This preliminary study of the Swedish affiliates of socialist multinationals has provided some useful information about the scale of the commercial activity of these organizations. In general, it appears that they are similar in scope of operation to their British counterparts, although smaller in terms of average turnover and size of fixed investment. As in the case of the United Kingdom the range of operations of these companies is consistent with the profile of their parent foreign trade organizations, whilst their comparative small-ness can be accounted for by the Swedish market being smaller than its British counterpart.

(ii)   The majority of Swedish affiliates of socialist multinationals do not appear to perform particularly well in terms of profits in relation to turnover or fixed assets, although there are some exceptions. This conclusion is based on their similarities in profitability performance to British affiliates of socialist multi-nationals and the fact that these British affiliates in turn do not compare well with other British companies on this indicator. Consequently, it appears that the objectives of both Swedish and British affiliates are related more to turnover than profitability, although clearly these indicators will have been adversely influenced by macroeconomic conditions in both countries.

(iii)   It is considered important to supplement this preliminary study by case study research similar to that included in the previous chapter on British companies. Tungsram AB and Matreco Handels AB present themselves as obvious candidates for such research.

(iv)   It is suggested that the role played by Sweden's neutrality in East–West trade in general, and the operation of Swedish affiliates of socialist multinationals in particular, be considered as a topic for further research. The Swedish market-place in general may be more open to socialist-manufactured goods and socialist investment, and the absence of the necessity of observing Cocom[8] requirements (since Sweden is not a member of NATO) may give rise to an easier two-way flow of trade. If trade is generally freer between Sweden and the socialist countries, the Swedish affiliates may have important roles to play in the servicing of this trade.

Notes and references

1. For convenience, those Swedish-based companies which contain Soviet and Eastern European investment capital have been referred to as 'affiliates of socialist multinationals in Sweden'.
2. C.H. McMillan and P. Egyed (eds), *East–West Business Directory: A Listing of Companies in the West with Soviet and East European Equity Participation*, Duncan Publishing, London, 1983.
3. Private letter, Exchange Control Department, Sveriges Riksbank, Stockholm, 24 August 1982.
4. Nordic Bank plc provided a Beijerinvest pamphlet, *A Reader's Guide to Swedish Financial Statements* (AB Custodia, Stockholm, 7th edn. 1981), which has been used to gain an understanding of Swedish company accounting practices, together with *Starting a Business in Sweden*, Svenska Handelsbanken, January 1980.
5. C.E. Pratten, *A Comparison of the Performance of Swedish and UK Companies*, University of Cambridge, Department of Applied Economics, Occasional Paper No.47, Cambridge University Press, 1976.
6. Ibid.
7. Inter-Company Comparisons (ICC) Limited, *Industrial Performance Analysis: A Financial Analysis of UK Industry and Commerce*, ICC Business Ratios Division, London, 1981.
8. Cocom (Co-ordinating Committee) includes all NATO members with the exception of Iceland, plus Japan. The Committee exists primarily to co-ordinate the trade policies of the Western allies towards the socialist countries of Eastern Europe, particularly for those products having strategic importance.

4 Soviet and Eastern European Firms in the Federal Republic of Germany

Peter Knirsch

The attitude of the CMEA states [1] to foreign capital investment

The ideological position

While a pluralistic approach to societal and economic phenomena is both possible and usual in Western countries, in the Soviet Union and the socialist countries of Eastern Europe intellectual life is very clearly influenced by the official ideology based on Marxism-Leninism. This also applies to the approach to international economic relations in general and to capital investment abroad in particular. It is not disputed that the significance of international economic relations based on an increasingly specialized international division of labour has grown in the last decades. In Eastern Europe it is assumed that this is so both in the area where that system prevails which is classified as 'socialism'[3] and in the area of what is termed 'capitalism', that of the Western industrialized nations.[4]

So far as capitalism is concerned, not only a growth in international economic relations — by this is meant trade, production, payment, and credit relations[5] — but also an 'internationalization of capital' is regarded as typical of the present economic development. It is assumed, based on the views of Lenin,[6] that in 'imperialism', as the present stage of capitalist development is called, national barriers to capital are lifted; the structure of the developed Western industrialized nations and the relations between them are essentially determined by 'international monopolies'.[7] The role of these international monopolies — basically they correspond to those enterprises which in the West are referred to as 'multinationals' — in the world economy and in world affairs is seen as thoroughly negative.[8] From the point of view of their economic significance, the problem is perceived to be their 'control' of a significant part of foreign trade as well as of the world's industrial production and raw materials exploitation; thus they are able to use their position of power to gain monopolistic profits. They are supported in this by the political and military power of their 'countries of origin', which in turn are largely dominated by the international monopolies, whereby their national sovereignty is limited.[9]

In the past two decades, and above all in the 1970s, the CMEA countries themselves have founded an increasing number of 'international economic organizations' which, as joint organizations of several states, also involve international capital ownership.[10] They have also made direct investments in individual development projects; essentially these were investments in the Soviet Union made by the smaller European CMEA countries for the purpose of exploiting and transporting raw material deposits.[11] In addition, a third form of CMEA participation in the 'internationalization of capital' also developed, again primarily during the 1970s: investments outside the CMEA itself, that is, in the Western industrialized countries and in the Third World. Investments of this kind in the Federal Republic of Germany represent the subject of this chapter, and those in Austria are treated in Chapter 5.

In comparison with international capital relations between Western countries, the extent of the CMEA countries' participation in the 'internationalization of capital' is extremely limited: both the number and still more the size of their international investments are considerably smaller. Nevertheless, the inclusion of investments in the international economic relations of the CMEA countries poses a certain ideological problem: the notion that foreign investments and international capital ownership are reprehensible would appear to the impartial observer to apply in principle to Soviet and East European foreign investments also. As far as we know, there have been no explicit discussions of this aspect; the works cited here assume as a matter of course that the same phenomenon has quite a different meaning in the context of the socialist system than it has under 'imperialism'.

The foreign investments of the CMEA countries are thus understood solely as a reinforcement of the international division of labour; the possibility of exercising economic and political influence through these capital investments is not discussed, nor is there any discussion of the problems of 'exploitation' associated with realizing profits in foreign countries. We can leave aside the question of whether this point of view is justifiable in the case of capital investments among the CMEA countries, that is, within their own system. In the case of the inter-systemary capital investments we are concerned with here, this viewpoint appears untenable: the function of these investments is to strengthen the position of the CMEA countries in the Western world market. This means that because of these foreign investments higher foreign trade profits can be made than would otherwise have been possible.

This aim does not differ from the capitalist countries' motives for exporting capital. But this capitalist approach to the use of capital in foreign countries is regarded in Soviet political economy as a negative — indeed a reprehensible — characteristic of imperialism.

> The export of capital abroad has as its aim the realization of monopoly profits.

> The export of capital is closely connected with the growth of commodity exports: the monopolies which export capital generally force the debtor countries to buy their wares — moreover on conditions which are extremely advantageous to the monopolies. The foreign monopolies appropriate for themselves the markets and the national resources of the debtor countries.

> The export of capital has serious consequences for the capital-exporting countries. These countries multiply . . . their wealth and strengthen their position on the world market. They receive a steady stream of surplus value in the form of interest on loans or profits from the enterprises abroad . . .[12]

These polemic words are to be found in a Soviet textbook which was once widely read. We certainly do not believe that these conclusions have any immediate relevance to present-day CMEA investments in the West and in the developing countries. Nevertheless, it should not be forgotten — and hence the need for this excursion into political economy — that the decision makers in the Soviet Union and in the other CMEA states who are responsible for foreign investment have learnt these very words about the export of capital and foreign investments. It would be most remarkable if these ideas — perhaps unconsciously — were not to play a role in their reflections on their own capital investments.

Limits to and prospects for CMEA foreign investment

In practice, however, the ideological dilemma of the CMEA countries with regard to their inter-systemary foreign investment has had little significance in the last few years. This is because their foreign investments have so far been very limited, as our specific examples will show. Admittedly, in our country studies we come to the conclusion that the CMEA countries' investments — at least their investments outside their own system —are made to strengthen their foreign trade position or to realize profits abroad in precisely the same manner as, according to the polemic formulation of their ruling ideology quoted earlier, is typical of the negative characteristics of the Western industrialized nations. It would be meaningless, however, given the present level of Soviet and Eastern European investments in the West, to speak of the possibility of 'monopoly profits' being realized or markets conquered in this way. This is at least valid with regard to the significance of these investments in Western industrialized countries; a similar investigation of specific developing countries might lead to a different assessment of the role of CMEA investments.

It may be assumed that the economic policy-makers in the CMEA countries are well aware of the relatively minor significance of their investments in the West. The main reasons for this are, as we shall show in more detail later, the capital shortage suffered by all CMEA countries and their shortage also of the convertible currencies needed for investments in the West. Both factors set clear limits to the CMEA countries' foreign investment.

The fact that no general discussion of the possibilities and problems of foreign investment is to be found in the economic literature of the CMEA countries may be due to the ideological implications. A slim pamphlet for economic practitioners, published by the Romanian Chamber of Commerce and Industry, identifies the aims of mixed trading companies as being:[13]

— to increase the volume of Romanian commodity exports;
— to diversify exports;
— to gain a foothold in new markets;
— to improve import and export prices and conditions of payment in import and export;
— to guarantee new sources of raw materials;
— to realize net profits in foreign currency through commercial or financial operations;

— to gain first-hand knowledge of markets and of the exploitation
   of factors connected with trade cycles;
— to adapt Romanian products to the demands of the market with
   regard to technology, quality, presentation and packaging;
— to sell directly to the ultimate consumer;
— to exploit customs facilities and tax relief;
— to train Romanian personnel.

The pamphlet proceeds from the assumption that in 1981 about 14
per cent of Romanian exports to developed Western countries and to
the developing countries were marketed through such mixed
companies, and that the number and the activities of such companies
are to increase in the future.

   In various conversations with foreign trade experts from CMEA
countries, too, a very positive assessment of the possibilities for
foreign investments in the West was given. In present conditions,
where very little information on this matter is forthcoming, it is not
possible to say whether such views are representative of general
opinion in the CMEA and whether they are politically relevant.

   Nevertheless, in making an assessment of the CMEA's investments
in the West, it is important to know that such views are held by
experts from the East. Thus it would appear possible that efforts to
expand such investments will increase in the future. The general state
of East–West economic relations, above all East–West trade and
credit relations, is a source of little satisfaction at present; for this very
reason, it is possible that greater emphasis will be placed on foreign
trade investment. Of the restrictive factors identified earlier, the
capital shortage is undoubtedly only relative, that is, it exists only due
to the conditions currently prevailing in the CMEA countries. An
international comparison shows that the ratio of domestic investment
to national income is high in these countries, but investment
efficiency, which is too low, and declining capital productivity are the
subject of frequent criticism in the CMEA. Given appropriate
conditions in the world economy, it could be worthwhile for these
countries to reflect upon the alternative course of making some of
these investments in Western industrialized countries or in developing countries, where efficiency would be greater. A solution to the
currency problem appears at first sight to be more difficult. However,
if we bear in mind that a very considerable amount of convertible
currency must be expended on possibly rather expensive imports of
raw materials, half-finished goods, and modern technology, and that

under the specific conditions of the system the use of these imported goods is often inefficient, then the use of a part of this foreign exchange for profitable capital investment abroad would certainly appear economically worthwhile.

Of course, such considerations are highly speculative. If they are to be realized, above all a considerable change in the CMEA countries' political approach to economic relations with the West will be necessary. It is not possible to make any well-founded statement as to the probability of such changes. Nevertheless, it appears that the tendency will in the longer term be towards increasing CMEA investments in the West and that the cases of foreign investment and foreign companies presented in the following pages will prove to be the historic forerunners of a new and increasingly important phenomenon in international economic relations.

CMEA enterprises in the Federal Republic of Germany

This section examines the firms and holdings of the seven European CMEA states* in the Federal Republic of Germany and West Berlin. Investments by the non-European CMEA countries and by other socialist countries are not considered. Of these, Yugoslav investments are of relatively great importance; in addition, we have learnt during the course of our research of nine firms belonging to the People's Republic of China in the Federal Republic of Germany. These were not included in this study, however, since it is limited to an examination of direct investments by the European CMEA countries.

Forms of investment

Included in this study are those firms located in the Federal Republic of Germany whose entire working capital comes from the European CMEA countries or which were founded or are operated as 'mixed enterprises' ('joint ventures') by CMEA countries in partnership with West German and/or other Western investors. The Eastern European

---

* These comprise the Soviet Union, the German Democratic Republic, Czechoslovakia, Bulgaria, Romania, Hungary and Poland.

Table 4.1 *Possible types of CMEA participation in the West*

1. Participation by CMEA countries	2. Participation by Western countries
A. 100 per cent CMEA firm	
100 per cent CMEA capital	No Western participation
B. Mixed firm (joint venture)	
CMEA participation:	Western participation:
1a. Participation by foreign trade organizations of a country	2a. Participation by a German partner (individual or company)
1b. Participation by enterprise associations of a country	2b. Participation by several German partners (individual or company)
1c. Participation by a single state-owned enterprise of a country (especially banks, insurance companies, transport firms)	2c. Participation by partners from the Federal Republic of Germany and other Western countries
1d. Participation by the respective firms or organizations of several CMEA countries	2d. No German participation; participation by partners from other Western countries
1e. Indirect participation of CMEA countries through a CMEA firm based in the West or through CMEA participation in a firm based in the West	

investments are always made by state-owned enterprises, in accordance with the economic systems of these countries. State foreign trade organizations represent the great majority of Eastern European investors, but at the same time there are also investments by enterprise associations and by individual state-owned firms (see Table 4.1).

In this study as many Eastern European investors as possible were taken into consideration, but their inclusion here should by no means be taken to mean that they are comparable to Western multinationals. Only the cases where Eastern European participation is openly reported could be considered. The possibility cannot be ruled out that other firms from CMEA countries also participate in West German firms as secret partners. However, we have the impression that the share represented by such investments is not very large.

One difficulty that arises in limiting the scope of the study is distinguishing between the state firms that operate in the West and the official trade delegations which are usually associated with the embassies of the respective CMEA countries, where representatives of the state foreign trade associations are also active. Except for the Office of Soviet Foreign Trade Associations in the Western Sectors of Berlin, which is operative in concluding foreign trade transactions, we have not included official trade delegations in this survey.

On the other hand, the study does include agencies of foreign trade organizations and branch offices of service enterprises of the CMEA countries, such as airline companies, freight companies, and banks. One can hardly speak of 'investment' in such cases, for such firms have only business premises at their disposal; they possess no capital stock. If we assume that CMEA firms in the West represent a fairly recent phenomenon whose development in the future could well be dynamic, it seems reasonable to include all firms in the study for they can provide a starting-point for further developments. In addition, the data presented here frequently do not permit a clear distinction between agencies on the one hand and companies on the other.

Motives for investment by CMEA countries in the West

The founding of firms in the West by state-owned enterprises from the CMEA countries or the participation of these countries in Western firms is a relatively recent phenomenon. With the exception of a few rather exotic cases which have a historical explanation, most of these firms have come into existence during the past ten to fifteen years. Since all the CMEA countries are striving to make extensive domestic investments as a consequence of their development strategy, it can be presumed that they may potentially lack capital for foreign investment. Considerations of more extensive foreign capital investment have probably had no significance in the economic policy of these countries so far, no doubt in part because any such considerations would also be subject to strong ideological reservations.

In addition to this, all the CMEA countries included in this study suffer from a chronic shortage of hard currency reserves that has already made it extremely difficult for them to satisfy their current needs for imports from the hard currency countries. In this situation expansion of foreign trade with the Western industrial nations has only been possible on the basis of Western credits such as were granted during the 1970s. Up to now, this unfavourable balance of payments situation has made the very idea that the CMEA countries would be able to make more extensive capital investments in Western industrial countries seem Utopian.

Nevertheless it was precisely this unfavourable balance of payments *vis-à-vis* the hard currency countries that provided the most important motivation for the CMEA countries to make direct investments in the Western industrial nations, although on a generally modest scale: the companies established or partnerships entered into for this reason are intended above all to promote the export of Soviet and Eastern European goods to the West, to reduce the (hard currency) costs associated with these exports, or to produce hard currency revenues. Consequently *trading firms* for the distribution of Soviet and Eastern European export products predominate among the CMEA firms in the Federal Republic of Germany. Along with preparing the ground for and carrying out business transactions, the marketing of their respective products and the establishment of their own customer services and warehouses are of primary importance.

The alternative to the CMEA countries' own trading firms is cooperation with independent German commercial agencies and import firms. These commercial agencies normally operate at their own expense and for a commission. They have a good knowledge of the market and have already expended a great deal of effort to establish relationships with appropriate buyers. Occasionally Eastern European countries have founded companies of their own in order to save some or all of the commission fees of these commercial agencies. As an intermediary stage, joint firms are frequently founded. In many such cases the German commercial agencies are offered a partnership in the firm. In less favourable cases an offer is made to hire the commerical agent as a salaried employee. At worst, the contract is cancelled on the date when it becomes legally possible to terminate it. Compensation payments are only made if they are provided for by the contract. This transformation of former commercial agencies into trading firms completely or partly owned by CMEA countries is also to the latter's advantage to the extent that their export activity for individual categories of goods is thereby centralized.

The *service enterprises* of the CMEA countries which operate in the Federal Republic of Germany (chiefly transport companies, banks, and insurance companies) are intended to reduce hard currency costs for Soviet and Eastern European export and import firms by making it unnecessary to utilize the respective services of the Western service sector. In addition, these enterprises are also supposed to produce direct revenues in hard currency by developing their own business activities in the West. There are repeated complaints by Western partners in East–West trade that Soviet and Eastern European buyers try to prescribe utilization of their own service enterprises, especially in the case of transport companies and banks.

While promoting exports and earning hard currency by providing services represent the main reasons for Soviet and Eastern European investments in the West, there are also some motives of secondary importance: to a certain extent the CMEA firms serve to provide training for professionals who thus become directly acquainted with Western market conditions. It is also not without significance that an assignment in the West represents a kind of reward to CMEA staff members for their professional abilities or, also, for political good behaviour, and often serves as an important stepping stone in their careers. The business activity of CMEA firms in the Federal Republic of Germany does, however, suffer because the CMEA staff members are transferred rather frequently, on average after one to five years. In particular, mixed companies complain that such frequent transfers interfere with the continuity of business activity.

Soviet and Eastern European firms with their headquarters in the Federal Republic of Germany are also involved — though to a considerably lesser extent — with handling the imports of the CMEA countries. The cost advantages which can be realized through such a concentration of demand may explain this activity. In view of the anticipated intensification of Western embargo measures, it will be interesting to see whether CMEA firms located in the West become more active in CMEA import transactions, especially since these firms are also associated with corresponding firms in European countries which are not members of NATO (Austria, Sweden, and Switzerland).

The view that the mixed companies of the CMEA countries employ members of Eastern bloc secret services, which is asserted again and again in Western news media, is not verifiable.[14] There is supposedly no connection between these firms and the West German Communist Party (DKP). It is claimed in a press report that Bulgarian, Czechoslovak, Polish, and Hungarian state enterprises all have holdings in the firm Plambeck u. Co. Druck und Verlag GmbH in Neuss, which is allegedly sympathetic to the DKP and whose profits are possibly used to finance the DKP.[15] We did not come across this firm in the course of our research and we have not included it in our list of mixed companies, although as a unique example of a common investment by several CMEA countries, it would certainly be an interesting special case.

Basis for and difficulties in carrying out the empirical study

The purpose of this study was to provide a survey of the firms operating in the Federal Republic of Germany with Soviet and Eastern European capital and to gather as much information as possible on their activities. We discovered during the course of our research that direct investments by CMEA countries have not been systematically recorded by any institution in the Federal Republic of Germany. At the same time all the institutions contacted expressed intense interest in the results of such a study, and in this respect the need of economic practitioners for information of this sort is apparently very great.

Under these circumstances, a great deal of work was required and it was an extremely arduous task to compile a more or less complete survey of CMEA firms. Given the limitations of time and finance, it proved possible to provide only a general outline of the situation.

During the course of our research a systematic approach was employed, and we began by sending a questionnaire to all sixty-nine Chambers of Commerce in the Federal Republic of Germany and West Berlin. However, an examination of the completed questionnaires revealed that the Chambers of Commerce are by no means always able to provide a complete listing of all firms operating with CMEA capital in their areas of competence. This information was therefore supplemented by addressing enquiries to the foreign trade organizations of the CMEA countries involved in the survey, which are to be regarded as the most important Soviet and Eastern European investors. The number of questionnaires returned was not very satisfactory (about ten organizations provided — in some cases fairly detailed — information).

While this part of the empirical study may still be designated as 'systematic', it was necessary to supplement the information obtained by these two methods by reviewing business reports and by studying announcements in the daily press about relevant transactions, entries in trade registers, reports in foreign trade journals, and reports and announcements in West German technical journals. In the time available it was only possible to review such publications on a random basis.

Older studies by Carl H. McMillan[16] and R. Bruce Morgan,[17] as well as a pamphlet published by the Romanian Chamber of Commerce and Industry[18] and a circular put out by the Ost-Ausschuss der Deutschen Wirtschaft,[19] represented valuable additions to our material. In addition, lists of Bulgarian and Polish firms and holdings in Western countries, drawn up by these two countries' Chambers of Commerce, were at our disposal.

All these random sources, which differ widely so far as their origin and methods are concerned, are alike in being incomplete to a greater or lesser extent. The number of firms covered is in every case considerably smaller than in our systematic inquiry. We have attempted to compile as complete a survey as possible by summarizing these various sources. In so doing, we have also included firms whose existence could not be ascertained beyond all doubt.

In connection with this approach, it should be borne in mind that in principle fairly detailed data on all firms in the Federal Republic of Germany are available: particulars about them can be examined in the local trade registers. The year a firm was founded, the names of the liable partners and the nominal amounts of capital for which they are liable, the names of the firms' authorized representatives, and the companies' statutes, together with the objectives of each enterprise, can all be identified from these registers, which are maintained by the competent local courts (*Amtsgerichte*) and are accessible to the public. Since, with three exceptions, we knew the registered location (*Firmensitz*) of each firm with CMEA ownership or participation, in principle it should have been possible to obtain this information. However, such a method of procedure would have necessitated personal visits to the respective local courts, involving a considerable outlay in time and money. Moreover, since the information contained in the trade registers is somewhat limited and does not include such economically important data as actual/real capital, turnover, profits, and number of employees, we felt it reasonable to dispense with gathering details from the trade register for the present study; the cost would probably have outweighed any potential gains.

The results of the empirical study

Altogether, 157 enterprises of the state-trading countries that conduct business in the Federal Republic of Germany or represent business interests there were included in the study. As far as can be seen from

the literature cited earlier, the CMEA countries thus have more firms
and holdings in the Federal Republic of Germany than in any other
Western country. Probably this is chiefly due to the fact that the Federal
Republic of Germany, at least among the larger Western countries,
has the closest economic relations with the CMEA. A second reason
may be the geographical proximity of the Federal Republic of
Germany to the individual CMEA countries. The fact that in the
Federal Republic of Germany the regulations governing the
establishment of a business are quite liberal and uncomplicated may
also play a part.

The degree of involvement by individual CMEA countries in
owning enterprises in the Federal Republic of Germany or openly
holding interests in West German firms varies greatly. Table 4.2
shows that Poland heads the CMEA countries with fifty-three such
enterprises. The second and third places are occupied by Hungary
and the Soviet Union, which have recently shown renewed interest in
strengthening their position on the West German market by
establishing branch offices or participating in mixed companies.
Then follows Bulgaria, which also wants to intensify its activities in
the Federal Republic of Germany. Czechoslovakia too is showing
increased interest with regard to future investment. On the other
hand, at present Poland and Romania are not known to be planning
or implementing increased investments — they are probably hardly
in a position to do so, given their domestic problems and their heavy
indebtedness to the West.

Table 4.2 *CMEA company activity in the Federal Republic of
Germany, 1982*

Country	No. of firms with CMEA ownership or participation	as % of total
Bulgaria	20	13
Czechoslovakia	12	8
Hungary	31	19
Poland	53	34
Romania	12	8
Soviet Union	29	18
Total	157	100

In this listing it is striking that it has not been possible to find a single firm in the Federal Republic of Germany that is either owned by the German Democratic Republic or in which the GDR has a partial interest. Discussions with experts on this subject produced contradictory information about two companies, which could not be included in our list.

Investments by CMEA countries have been made primarily in the large trading and industrial centres in the western and northern parts of the Federal Republic of Germany, while so far southern Germany has not been as strongly represented (see Table 4.3). It is clear that Frankfurt and Hamburg, followed by Düsseldorf and Cologne, are strongly favoured as locations for companies or holdings of the state-trading nations. In contrast, southern Germany is the location for more of the Yugoslav-owned firms or firms with Yugoslav participation, which are not included in this study.

A closer examination of the addresses of these companies reveals that, in many cases, several firms in which a CMEA country has holdings all have the same address: the offices of these firms are to be found in one building. This indicates that, in such cases, we are dealing with relatively small firms which do not need large premises. It may also signify that some of these firms, which are legally independent of each other, work in close cooperation.

Table 4.3   *Regional distribution of CMEA investment in the Federal Republic of Germany, 1982*

| Location | No. of companies with CMEA ownership or participation | | | | | | |
	Bulgaria	Czecho-slovakia	Hungary	Poland	Romania	Soviet Union	Total
Frankfurt-on-Main	8	5	9	7	4	7	40
Hamburg	1	2	1	16	1	5	26
Düsseldorf	—	2	—	12	1	2	17
Cologne	—	—	3	7	1	4	15
Berlin (West)	2	—	1	2	—	8	13
Munich	1	—	5	—	1	1	8
Stuttgart	2	—	1	—	1	—	4
Other locations	5	3	10	9	2	2	31
Unknown	1	—	1	—	1	—	3
							157

Determining the registered location (Firmensitz) of a firm is important, since only by so doing does it become possible to gather further details on the companies from the appropriate trade registers. In the case of three firms, it was not possible to trace the registered location.

Our study produced concrete information not previously compiled about the areas of activity engaged in by firms with CMEA ownership or participation in the Federal Republic of Germany, since we were able to ascertain the nature of most of the companies' business. The range of goods and services offered is extremely wide. In principle, it reflects the entire scope of the goods and services provided by the CMEA countries in question and to this extent it does not provide any new insights, especially since the declared business purposes simply characterize possible areas of activity. These areas are by no means fully exploited in every case.

As can be seen from Table 4.4, of the 157 companies included in the study, eighty-two (52 per cent) are trading companies and twenty-six (17 per cent) are service enterprises, while only three firms are registered as production enterprises. Forty-six firms (29 per cent) were identified as agencies, and in these the distinction between a joint-stock company on the one hand and sole tradership or an agency on the other is not always clearly drawn in the relevant documents.

Our investigation of the *business activity* of CMEA-owned firms or firms with CMEA participation in the Federal Republic of Germany resulted — more or less coincidentally — in only a few scattered pieces of information. West German commercial law does not require such information to be published in the case of *GmbHs*

Table 4.4   *Areas of CMEA company activity in the Federal Republic of Germany, 1982*

	Trade	Services	Production	Agencies	Total
Bulgaria	9	2	2	7	20
Czechoslovakia	7	—	—	5	12
Hungary	20	5	—	6	31
Poland	29	6	—	18	53
Romania	5	4	1	2	12
Soviet Union	12	9	—	8	29
Total	82	26	3	46	157

(private limited companies) and sole traders; it therefore had to be gathered from a very few reports in economic journals. An account of the business activities of the three banks in which the state-trading nations have holdings, and which as *Aktiengesellschaften* (public limited companies) are required to publish business reports, balance sheets, and profit and loss accounts, is given later in this chapter. In the case of the other companies, the majority of which have the legal form of a *GmbH*, it is not possible to summarize the few individual pieces of information available in a meaningful form. It appears that most of these firms were founded in the 1970s; however, new firms are clearly being founded at the present time too, and the state-trading nations' interest in such companies appears to be unchanged.

The majority of the firms are comparatively small trading firms, although in a few cases there are reports of a considerable turnover. Several of the companies classified as trading companies also provide services, in that they assume responsibility for services relevant to the products they trade. Trade as the main activity is associated with production in a few cases where the firms also carry out the assembly or production of parts of the goods they trade.

Our research results in comparison with the state of international research

Although our research results leave many questions of detail concerning the business activity of CMEA firms open, they nevertheless represent considerable progress compared to the prior state of research. The most comprehensive study in this area to date by Carl H. McMillan refers to a total of fifty-four CMEA-owned firms or mixed companies with CMEA participation in the Federal Republic of Germany — by contrast, our listing of 157 is considerably more comprehensive. Since it was not possible to establish with any degree of certainty when these firms were founded, it cannot be said whether the older study was largely incomplete or whether the number of firms has risen sharply in the intervening four years. The fact that our criteria for including such firms were formulated more broadly (in particular, McMillan's study does not include the airline companies of the CMEA countries, which together with their branch offices account for fourteen firms) only slightly influenced the total number of firms included. We are inclined to the view that all these factors have contributed to the difference in the number of firms listed.

The list recently published by the Ost-Ausschuss der Deutschen Wirtschaft names a hundred firms with capital from CMEA countries; the study includes agencies. In this case too, the number of firms included is considerably smaller than in our study and, with the exception of business purposes, there is no information whatever on company activity.

Banks as a special form of CMEA firms and mixed companies operating in the Federal Republic of Germany

General information

The state-trading countries of Eastern and Central Europe make use of various possibilities in order to gain a foothold in Western markets. One important way in which they do this is by founding their own firms or participating in mixed companies in Western industrial nations, including the Federal Republic of Germany and West Berlin. Among such firms and mixed companies can be included the banks owned or part-owned by CMEA countries.

In the Federal Republic of Germany three such banks operate from the banking centre in Frankfurt am Main. These are the Frankfurt Bukarest Bank AG, with Romanian participation, the Mitteleuropäische Handelsbank Aktiengesellschaft, in which Poland holds shares, and the Ost-West-Handelsbank AG, which is financed solely by Soviet capital.

The transactions conducted by the banks of the eastern and south-eastern European state-trading countries operating in the Federal Republic of Germany are greatly influenced by the situation of these countries with regard to trade with the West. Since these banks are concerned primarily with foreign trade transactions, i.e. with financing bilateral merchandise movement, their volume of business is relatively limited. They make their profits by negotiating documentary credits (letters of credit and collections). German commercial banks, on the other hand, derive their income from transactions in securities and credit transactions. While German banks do 80 per cent of their refinancing through customer deposits and only 20 per cent through bank deposits, in the case of the foreign banks cited here the relationship is just the opposite, 10 per cent as against 90 per cent.

This different structure of the Eastern European banks (relatively modest capital resouces, no network of branch offices, relative insignificance of customer deposits) is also reflected in their balance sheet totals. While in 1982 the German Dresdner Bank AG had a balance sheet total of approximately DM80,000m (excluding shares in German and foreign subsidiaries), the largest of the CMEA banks, the Ost-West-Handelsbank AG of Frankfurt am Main, had a balance sheet total of only DM2,000m. Thus the banks operating in the Federal Republic of Germany with Eastern European partici-pation are about the same size as a number of private banks in Germany, for example:

Bankhaus Trinkaus & Burkhardt, Cologne	DM 4,000m
Bankhaus Sal. Oppenheim, Cologne	DM 3,000m
Bankhaus Warburg, Brinkmann & Wirtz, Hamburg	DM 2,000m
Bankhaus Schröder, Münchmeyer, Hengst & Co., Frankfurt and Hamburg	DM 2,000m

Experts in this area are unanimous in their assessment of the goals that these Eastern European banks pursue. The state-trading countries are primarily concerned with participating in banking transactions in the Federal Republic of Germany and earning commissions in foreign currency. In so doing, they operate according to purely business considerations and try to make as large a profit as possible. Furthermore, it seems to be important to these countries to gain a foothold in the West German banking business. They are also interested in sending their banking experts to Western countries so that they can study the 'capitalist' banking mechanism and learn how the various aspects of the Western banking system are interrelated. Frequently these countries wish to carry out individual transactions which require knowing the 'rules of the game' for the Western banking system.[20]

The question that comes to mind in this connection — to what extent do these banks influence West Germany's East–West trade? — can be answered in part by pointing out that the respective Eastern European countries require that their banks be used to handle financial transactions. For example, in their sales contracts the foreign trade organizations of the Soviet Union stipulate the banking connection, in other words the Ost-West-Handelsbank AG, so that it can collect the bank commission. By this means West German banks are often kept from participating in the transactions. By contrast, West German banks are only authorized to have representative offices in the state-trading countries. This means that they are not allowed to conclude transactions, but rather may only look after their 'regular customers'.

The three Eastern European banking institutions cited have the character of being purely settling banks. These mixed companies are limited in the financing of transactions, since they are not syndicate members of the German AKA (Ausfuhr- und Kreditanstalt GmbH, the German credit institution for exports) which, working together with the exporters' 'house banks', refinances German exports.

Originally all three also intended to participate in non-recourse financing (the institution concerned does not accept liability for transactions for which it acts as an intermediary). However, since the credit-worthiness of the state-trading countries has been negatively affected for some time now by their indebtedness in the West and unfavourable economic developments, these banks no longer wish to participate in non-recourse financing transactions.

West German law places no restrictions on the three banks: they all have unrestricted banking licences. They would undoubtedly be in a position to carry out larger-scale business transactions if they were better supplied with capital resources.

In addition to the commercial banks with Eastern European capital, there are also the representative offices of the Eastern European banks at the banking centre of Frankfurt am Main, which, however, do not have banking licences. Their task is to maintain contacts with public institutions, banks, and trade and industrial groups. They are not mixed companies, but instead are completely owned by the respective state-trading countries. One of these is the representative office of the Ceskoslovenská Obchodni Banka AS located at Bochenheimer Landstrasse 51/53 and headed by a Czech citizen who at the same time is also a member of the managing board at the main office in Prague. The situation is similar at the representative office of the Ungarische Nationalbank at Frieden-strasse 4 and that of the Bulgarische Aussenhandelsbank on Grosse Bochenheimer Strasse 21.

In the following pages more detailed information about the business activities of the three Eastern European commercial banks will be provided. It is based on the 1981 annual report of the Ost-West-Handelsbank AG in Frankfurt am Main, the 1980 annual report of the Mitteleuropäische Handelsbank Aktiengesellschaft, and the 1981 annual report of the Frankfurt Bukarest Bank.

The Mitteleuropäische Handelsbank Aktiengesellschaft, Frankfurt am Main (1980)

The principal shareholders of the Mitteleuropäische Handelsbank Aktiengesellschaft are the Bank Handlowy w Warszawie S.A. (ul. Chaturbińskiego 8, Warsaw) and the Hessische Landesbank (Girozentrale) (Junghofstrasse 18–26, Frankfurt am Main).

If we discount the staff representatives, two German and four Polish citizens occupy positions on the supervisory board (*Aufsichstrat*). All six staff representatives of the supervisory board are of German nationality.

The managing board consists of two persons: the chairman is a Polish citizen, the other member being a German citizen. There are also four directors, of whom three are German citizens, with responsibility for loans, money and foreign exchange dealing, and accounting. The Polish director is responsible for documentary credit and payment transactions.

The bank has a share capital of DM40m, of which the principal shareholders hold the following shares:

Bank Handlowy w Warszawie — almost 70 per cent

Hessische Landesbank (Girozentrale) — 30 per cent

The Mitteleuropäische Bank acts chiefly as an intermediary, financing trade between the Federal Republic of Germany and Poland. In addition, the bank handles money transfers arising from import and export payments.

In 1980 rediscounting of bills of exchange and guarantee transactions amounted to almost DM1,000m. The bank's claims against non-banking institutions, together with bills in hand and endorsement liabilities, amounted to about DM370m. Included in the bank's claims against financial institutions are claims in connection with commercial credit transactions, largely through the bank's involvement with the financing of foreign trade in Western and Eastern European countries. Because of such connections elsewhere, the liabilities of the Mitteleuropäische Handelsbank include a considerable share of genuine deposit transactions with both non-banking and financial institutions.

The bank mainly grants loans to West German importers and exporters and to foreign buyers of goods, suppliers, and banks. Besides large firms, small and medium-sized enterprises are also among the bank's customers. As well as commercial credits, the bank also grants loans for financing the import of investment goods. In this area it works closely with other banks at the consortium level. The guarantee transactions of the bank consist largely of underwriting the risks of other banks participating in foreign consortiums for international Euro-credits.

In payment transactions the bank is active in handling import and export payments, mainly between the Federal Republic of Germany and Poland. Because of its familiarity with Polish foreign trade and with the foreign exchange and banking systems in both countries, the bank offers appropriate assistance in arranging bank payment orders.

The interest surplus was higher in the 1980 financial year than in 1979. This was due to the higher interest rates for capital investments and to the greater volume of the bank's own credits. Precaution against credit risks was taken by means of value adjustments. The remaining annual profit enabled the bank to pay a dividend of 7 per cent in 1980. The bank is a member of the Bankenverband Hessen e.V., Frankfurt, which belongs to the Bundesverband deutscher Banken e.V., Cologne.

In January 1980 the bank's share capital was raised nominally by DM12m to DM40m. On 4 January 1980 the bank called up and received one-half of the above-mentioned capital increase, together with the entire premium, amounting to 5 per cent of DM12m, and on 8 January 1981 it received the remaining sum of DM6m. The premium of DM600,000 was added in its entirety to the statutory reserves. The liable capital resources of the bank thus amounted to DM43.5m at the beginning of 1981.

The Ost-West-Handelsbank, AG Frankfurt am Main (1981)

The bodies with decision-making powers in this bank, which is in Soviet ownership, are the supervisory board (Aufsichtsrat) and the managing board; in addition to these, there are general agents and directors. The supervisory board has six members, of whom four apparently have Soviet citizenship and two are citizens of the Federal Republic of Germany. Two of the four members of the managing board are Soviet citizens: the chairman and the deputy chairman; the

others are West Germans. To judge by their names, two of the three
general agents are Soviet citizens and the third is a West German;
among the seven directors, one is a Soviet citizen and the remaining
six are of German nationality.

The shareholders of the Ost-West-Handelsbank AG are all Soviet
banks and Soviet foreign trade organizations. Their holdings are as
follows:

State Bank of the Soviet Union, Moscow	15.40%
Bank for Foreign Trade of the Soviet Union, Moscow	13.24%
State Savings Banks for Workers of the Soviet Union, Moscow	8.92%
V/O Almazjuvelirexport, Moscow	8.92%
V/O Exportles, Moscow	8.92%
V/O Promsyrioimport, Moscow	8.92%
V/O Sojuzgazexport, Moscow	8.92%
V/O Sojuzkoopvneshtorg, Moscow	8.92%
V/O Sudoimport, Moscow	8.92%
V/O Techmashimport, Moscow	8.92%

The bank's 1981 annual report outlines its progress. The general
economic situation remained difficult in 1981 as it had been in 1980,
so that the bank was obliged in 1981 (its ninth full business year) to
concentrate less on expanding the volume of business and more on
further strengthening its earnings capacity. Special attention was
therefore given to the service sector with the aim of increasing commission earnings from this sector. Through refinancing its lending business on largely similar terms, the bank was able to reap a safe interest
margin despite high initial costs. Moreover, it was generally possible to
adjust the interest rates on the asset side to the higher initial costs
through variable terms of payment.

The bank's volume of business — the balance sheet total together
with endorsement liabilities and bill guarantees — amounted to
DM2.17 thousand million, that is, DM52.3m (or 2.4 per cent) less than in
1980. The balance sheet total amounted to DM1.92 thousand million,
that is, DM65.6m (or 3.3 per cent) less than in 1980. With a volume of
business that only differed slightly from that of 1980 and with a 12 per
cent increase in operational costs, it was possible to increase the net
result by 81 per cent. No losses resulted from credit transactions;
however, precaution was taken against latent country risks.

The composition and scope of the credit transactions has changed very little. The fall in the volume of credit (the sum of the deposited bills of exchange, claims against customers, credits to banks, bill guarantees, and endorsement liabilities) in 1981 as against 1980 resulted entirely from a reduction of financial investments with terms of over three months and up to four years.

Altogether, there was again a slight increase in credits to banks and non-banking institutions. In view of the special structure of the bank's credit transactions, which consisted essentially of short- and medium-term foreign trade financing, a credit portfolio of virtually the same amount also implies that a considerable number of new credits have been granted to replace those that have been repaid.

Due to the rates of increase in letter of credit transactions and collecting business, and to increased yields in foreign payment transactions, commission yields increased by more than one-third as against 1980. The refinancing of the bank's lending business — essentially this was carried on with the bank's own monies — was guaranteed at all times. It was possible to increase the yields from dealing in money and also — despite turbulent foreign exchange markets — from foreign exchange dealings.

The volume of credit — bills of exchange, claims against customers, loans to banks (excluding claims of up to three months), bill guarantees, and endorsement liabilities — amounted to DM1.56 thousand million. This represents a reduction of DM0.25 thousand million (14 per cent) as against 1980. The individual items comprising the credit volume developed as follows in 1981: holdings of bills amounted to DM180.2m, of which DM176.7m were non-recourse discounted bills; endorsement liabilities from rediscounted bills rose from DM78m in 1980 to DM93.2m in 1981.

Within the volume of credit, customers' debts to the bank increased further. This item amounted to almost DM400m. The total debts of credit institutions were reduced by 7.3 per cent to DM1.19 thousand million. Within this item there was a shift away from debts with a term of at least three months to less than four years and towards debts with a term of less than three months. The item includes financial investments of DM997.7m, loans amounting to DM177m, and current assets and debts accruing to the bank through clearing transactions amounting to DM11.5m.

The bank's liquidity is described as satisfactory. Against liabilities totalling DM1.83 thousand million resulting from banking transactions with credit institutions and other customers, the bank's primary and secondary liquid funds amounted to DM1.2 thousand million. The cash reserves — cash in hand, deposits with the Bundesbank, postal cheque account deposits, together with cheques, interest, and dividend coupons — amounted to DM74.1m, that is, 51.6 per cent of the liabilities due at call (DM143.6m). Cash liquidity, i.e. the relation of cash reserves to total liabilities, amounted to 4.1 per cent. The total liquidity ratio amounted to 66 per cent.

The bank's holdings of securities amounted to DM73.7m. Loans and debenture stocks with a life of up to four years amounted to DM11.2m; securities with a life of over four years amounted to DM62.5m. The entire securities portfolio was eligible to serve as security for the Bundesbank. The Ost-West-Handelsbank continues to view its security holdings in their present volume as a long-term investment; above all, they are to ensure the bank's liquidity (with possibilities of use for lending on securities or for open market operations).

The Ost-West-Handelsbank AG has a number of holdings in other institutions, as shown in Table 4.5. The bank's fully paid-up share capital amounted to DM65m at the end of 1981. Together with declared reserves of DM20m, the bank's liable capital resources amounted to DM85m at the end of 1981.

At the end of 1981, the bank had a staff of ninety-five.

The Frankfurt Bukarest Bank AG, 1981

The Frankfurt Bukarest Bank AG is a mixed company with

Table 4.5   *Holdings of the Ost-West-Handelsbank AG*

	Capital	Share (%)
East–West United Bank S.A., Luxemburg	750 m. Lfr	4.67
Wozchod Handelsbank AG, Zürich	65 m. Sfr	3.85
Sobren Chemiehandel GmbH, Düsseldorf	DM 0.15 m.	2.00
Ost–West–Vermögensanlagen GmbH, Frankfurt am Main	DM 0.10 m.	100.00

Source: Annual Report, Ost–West Handelsbank AG, 1981.

Romanian, German, and French capital; the shareholders are the Rumänische Aussenhandelsbank of Bukarest (52 per cent), the Deutsche Genossenschaftsbank (DG-Bank) of Frankfurt am Main (24 per cent), the Berliner Handels- und Frankfurter Bank (BHF-Bank) of Frankfurt am Main (16 per cent), and the Banque Franco Roumaine of Paris (8 per cent).

The headquarters of the bank are located in Frankfurt am Main at Gutleutstrasse 45. Apparently, five Romanian and four German citizens work on the supervisory board. The members of the managing board are Cicerone Nitescu and Dr Gerhard Rohnfeld.

The main types of transactions conducted by the Frankfurt Bukarest Bank AG are foreign trade financing in Deutsche Mark and other currencies, documentary credit services for foreign trade transactions, and money-market business and foreign exchange dealings. In the area of documentary credits for foreign trade transactions, both the Frankfurt headquarters and also the branch office opened in Bucharest in 1980 have in the past mostly provided services to those customers involved in trade between the Federal Republic of Germany and Romania.

In 1981 trade between the Federal Republic of Germany and Romania was almost balanced, but trade volume decreased. Nevertheless, the bank was still able to increase its business activity, especially through the additional documentary credit transactions of the Bucharest branch. The total volume of documentary credit business was about 40 per cent higher than in 1980. This led to a 34 per cent increase in profits from commissions.

In 1981 the bank's business dealings were hindered by Romania's liquidity problems. The first reports of these appeared in 1981 according to the bank's 1981 annual report. However, the loans to Romanian borrowers were repaid according to the terms of the agreement, so that the mainly short-term Romanian commitments could for the most part be reduced in 1981. In March 1982 the Rumänische Aussenhandelsbank approached its creditors with a request for conversion of debts.

Compared to 1980, in 1981 the volume of business and the balance sheet total declined. The decisive factors in this development were the above-mentioned reduction of the Romanian liability and the restraint shown by the Frankfurt Bukarest Bank towards new transactions during the second half of the 1981 business year. A correspondingly reduced need for refinancing was associated with this. Despite increased precautions with regard to credit risks, in

1981 the Frankfurt Bukarest Bank was able to achieve an increase in annual net earnings.

Compared to the 1980 balance sheet, the bank's 1981 balance sheet total declined by DM102.3m to DM393.3m. This represents a 20.6 per cent decrease compared to 1980. The volume of business (balance sheet total plus contingent liabilities) amounted to DM564.1m and was DM80.6m (12.5 per cent) less than in the 1980 balance sheet.

While credit volume excluding contingent liabilities was reduced by DM103m (23.1 per cent), contingent liabilities increased by DM21.7m (14.6 per cent) due to the assumption of risks in the form of guarantees or credit orders for long-term Euro-currency financing. This also explains why the volume of business decreased less than the balance sheet sum. On the 1981 balance sheet, about 42 per cent of the credit volume was accounted for by customers in the Federal Republic of Germany and 58 per cent was broadly distributed among foreign borrowers. About one-fourth of the bank's credit volume was accounted for by borrowers in the state-trading countries, of which Romania's share was 12 per cent. The bank took appropriate precautions with regard to the Polish commitment, which represented 3.2 per cent of credit volume. At the end of 1981 the distribution and credit was practically unchanged, with 63 per cent accounted for by banks (of which short-term investments represented 29 per cent) and 37 per cent by non-banking institutions and bills of exchange.

The reduction in liabilities to credit institutions and other creditors by about DM103.4m was approximately equal to the decrease in the balance sheet total. On the 1981 balance sheet these liabilities amounted to DM355.1m; 90.6 per cent were liabilities to credit institutions and 9.4 per cent liabilities to other creditors. Among the obligations, the share represented by terms of over three months rose from 58.1 to 70.2 per cent.

The type of business done by the bank made it possible to keep non-interest-paying cash liquidity at quite a low level. Overall liquidity — cash liquidity, assets at credit institutions with terms of less than three months, as well as securities eligible to serve as collateral — amounted to DM122.8m and was thus DM21.3m, or 21 per cent, higher than on the 1980 balance sheet date.

On the 1981 balance sheet the bank's capital resources amounted to DM34.3m. This sum consisted of DM30m share capital (*Grund-kapital*) as well as DM3m in statutory reserves and DM1.3m in voluntary reserves; these capital resources were equivalent to 8.7 per cent of the balance sheet total of 6.1 per cent of business volume. The

Rumänische Aussenhandelsbank of Bucharest continues to hold a controlling interest (52 per cent) in the bank's share capital. The GEROM Beteiligungsgesellschaft mbH of Frankfurt am Main (in which the Deutsche Genossenschaftsbank holds a 60 per cent interest and the BHF-Bank 40 per cent) holds 40 per cent of the bank's shares.

The annual report gives the following information about the profit and loss account: the return on interest improved, since the interest margin grew and the average volume of business for the year was only slightly less than it had been in 1980. Specifically, interest income rose by DM12.2m (28 per cent), while the interest paid out by the bank increased by only DM10.3m (25.6 per cent). Thus the interest surplus amounted to DM5.1m. Profit from commissions also increased sharply, amounting to DM3.4m after expenditures on commissions are deducted. A substantial share of this increase — especially for the Bucharest branch — was due to commissions from providing documentary credits for foreign trade transactions, which accounted for just under 75 per cent of total earnings on commissions. The remaining 25 per cent of earnings from commissions came from guarantee and credit transactions.

Notes

1. This study takes into consideration the seven European states which work together in the CMEA (Council for Mutual Economic Assistance, often referred to in the West as 'Comecon'): the Soviet Union, Poland, the GDR, Czechoslovakia, Hungary, Romania, and Bulgaria. The three non-European members of the CMEA (Mongolia, Cuba, and Vietnam) have no significance in relation to our topic. Besides the designation 'CMEA states', the terms 'the East', 'Eastern Europe', and 'the socialist states of Eastern Europe', are also used to convey the same meaning.
2. In the context of this study, 'the West' refers to the developed Western industrialized countries which work together in the OECD.
3. Cf. for example Akademija Nauk SSSR, Institut Ekonomiki Mirovoj Socialisteceskoj Sistemy (ed.), *Proizvodstvennaja integracija stran SEV* (The Integration of Production in CMEA Countries), Moscow, 1972, p. 3 ff.
4. Cf. *Ökonomisches Lexikon* (Encyclopaedia of Economics), Vol. 1, East Berlin, 1967, p. 981.
5. Ibid., P. 981.
6. Cf. V.I. Lenin, 'Der Imperialismus als höchstes Stadium des Kapitalismus' (Imperialism as the Highest Stage of Capitalism), in *Ausgewählte Werke* (Selected Works), Vol. 1, East Berlin, 1954, pp. 767–875. Section

IV, 'Der Kapitalexport' (The Export of Capital), pp. 816–28, is of particular relevance to our topic.

7. The literature on this subject is very extensive. See, for example, Institut für Internationale Politik und Wirtschaft der DDR (ed.), *Internationale Monopole* (International Monopolies), East Berlin, 1978.

8. For a recent example, see Horst Heininger, 'Transnationale Konzerne und ihre schädliche Rolle in den internationalen Beziehungen' (Transnational Concerns and their Damaging Role in International Relations), in Gerhard Kade and Max Schmidt (eds.), *Frieden, Rüstung und Monopole*, Cologne, 1980, pp. 15–55.

9. For details of the views presented here in rough outline see the works cited in nn. 4 and 6.

10. This is treated in greater detail in Hans Bruder, Willi Kunz, and Siegfried Leidreiter, *Internationale ökonomische Organisationen der RGW-Länder* (International Economic Organizations of the CMEA Countries), East Berlin, 1980, especially pp. 128 ff.

11. See *Lexikon RGW* (CMEA Lexicon), Leipzig, 1981, pp. 109–112. Investments by one CMEA country in another CMEA country do not lead to the creation of enterprises having the legal form of joint (mixed) ventures; rather, such investments become the property of the country in which they are situated. The investments of the other CMEA countries have the form of an interest-bearing loan, which as a rule is repaid, together with interest, from the production of the jointly-established plant.

12. Thus the Akademie der Wissenschaften der UdSSR, Institut für Ökonomie (ed.), *Politische Ökonomie — Lehrbuch* (Political Economy — Textbook, (based on the 3rd, revised Russian edn.), East Berlin, 1959, pp. 252–4.

13. Handels- und Industriekammer der Sozialistischen Republik Rumänien (ed.), *Perspektiven für die Wirtschaftszusammenarbeit mit Rumänien durch gemischte Gesellschaften* (Prospects for Economic Cooperation with Romania through Mixed Companies), Bucharest, 1981, pp. 19 f. (direct quote, translated).

14. 'Östliche Agenten in deutschen Betrieben' (Eastern Agents in German Enterprises), *Frankfurter Allgemeine Zeitung*, 7 April 1982.

15. Ibid.

16. Carl H. McMillan, *Direct Soviet and East European Investment in the Industrialized Western Economies*, Working Paper No. 7, East–West Commercial Relations Series, Institute of Soviet and East European Studies, Carleton University, Ottawa, 1977, revised 1978.

17. R. Bruce Morgan and J. Reid Henry, *Directory of Soviet and East European Companies in the West*, Ottawa, Carleton University, 1979.

18. See n. 13.

19. 'Ost-Ausschuss der Deutschen Wirtschaft', mimeograph, Cologne, May 1982.

20. One example of this is the Moscow Narodny Bank in London (compared to London as the leading international European banking centre, Frankfurt is only a 'domestic' centre), where Soviet gold sales and share purchases take place 'out of the public eye'. In London such transactions are probably conducted 'invisibly' by a small group of insiders. London is also a favourite place for raising credit.

5 Soviet and East European firms in Austria

Peter Knirsch, in collaboration with *Jan Stankovsky*

Introduction

Austria's economic relations with the CMEA countries (as defined in Chapter 4) are closer than those of most Western industrial nations. The share of trade with the East in Austria's total foreign trade (12 – 15 per cent) is two or three times higher than in Western Europe. Austria's close trading relations with the state-trading nations are partly to be explained by geographical proximity, but also partly by the historical relations between Austria and the Eastern European states, which has facilitated mutual understanding.

Austria was one of the first Western countries to expand and supplement normal trading relations with industrial cooperation. Since the mid-1960s, a comparatively large number of cooperation agreements have been signed between enterprises in Austria and the CMEA countries.[1] Austria was also one of the first Western countries to sign treaties on tripartite cooperation — agreements between Eastern European, Western, and developing countries — with the state-trading nations.[2]

In connection with East–West economic relations, a special form of cooperation was at the centre of public interest from the very beginning: capital holdings of Western nations in enterprises in the CMEA countries (joint ventures) or in third countries, especially in developing countries. The complement to this form of cooperation — capital holdings of the CMEA countries in Western enterprises — attracted little attention.

This chapter aims to provide as comprehensive a survey as possible of CMEA capital holdings in Austrian enterprises. On the basis of the statistical material available, it was possible to draw conclusions about the forms of investment favoured by the CMEA countries and about the macroeconomic significance of their investments in Austria. A further purpose of the study was to gain clues as to the motives, aims, and objects behind such CMEA investments. The terms 'capital holdings', 'capital ownership', and 'direct investments' are used interchangeably.

Basis and limits of the study

In accordance with the aims of this study, all forms of CMEA ownership in Austrian enterprises were taken into consideration. This is true with regard both to the legal forms and to the percentage of capital owned by CMEA countries. Thus we included both enterprises which are 100 per cent CMEA owned, and enterprises in which the CMEA countries have majority or minority holdings; even minority owners can secure a decisive influence on enterprise activity for themselves. For the sake of linguistic simplicity in this chapter, all Austrian firms in which the CMEA countries have holdings are referred to as 'CMEA enterprises' or 'CMEA firms'.

The investigation revealed that, in Austria, the CMEA countries only participate in joint-stock companies (*Kapitalgesellschaften*), such as *Aktiengesellschaften* (AGs, or public companies) and *Gesellschaften mit beschränker Haftung* (GesmbHs or private companies), but not in *Einzelunternehmen* (sole traders) or partnership forms of organization such as *Offene Handelgesellschaften* (OHGs) or *Kommanditgesellschaften* (KGs).[3] The CMEA countries appear to avoid such forms of organization because, under Austrian law, the proprietors of *Einzelunternehmen* and such partnerships are liable to an unlimited extent.

CMEA capital ownership is clear in cases where CMEA enterprises (foreign trade organizations, banks, production enterprises) appear as capital owners. This category is referred to as *direct capital ownership* by the CMEA countries. The (comparatively infrequent) cases where a person domiciled in one of the CMEA countries appears as a capital owner were counted as direct capital ownership, since one may assume that such persons are agents of the actual owners. We also counted agencies (branch offices) of Eastern transport enterprises as CMEA firms, although in such cases there are no true capital investments in Austria and information on the employment of capital is also not available.[4]

Besides direct capital ownership, *indirect capital ownership* of the CMEA countries is also of interest. We use this term to describe CMEA participation in Austrian enterprises through other enterprises or persons, whereby multi-level arrangements are also possible. Of the various forms of indirect capital ownership, the following are of particular interest:

(a) An Austrian (or perhaps a citizen of another Western country) appears as the (sole or partial) owner of an Austrian enterprise, acting as a trustee for the actual Eastern European proprietor. It was not possible to identify such a form of indirect capital ownership during the course of the investigation, although it may be assumed that this form does exist.[5]

(b) Austrian enterprise A has a holding in another Austrian enterprise, B. A is owned by a CMEA country (indirect capital ownership via Austria). This form of indirect capital ownership was identified in a number of cases in the investigation; however, it is extremely difficult, especially when there are so many interlocking relationships, to collect data on such forms of participation, and our information is probably incomplete. A special form of indirect holding occurs in the case of companies with limited partnership. These forms have certain tax advantages for the main company. A *GesmbH*, often founded specifically for this purpose, acts as general partner. The CMEA countries generally participate in the *GesmbH und Co. KG* both directly (as limited partners in the *Kommanditgesellschaft*) and indirectly (as partners in the *GesmbH*).

(c) An enterprise from a third country, which is owned by a CMEA state, participates in an Austrian firm (indirect capital holding via a foreign country). Our investigation identified a number of cases of such indirect capital ownership, above all via Eastern European holding companies in Liechtenstein and Switzerland.[6] In the case of this form of indirect Eastern European capital ownership too, there could be a grey area, possibly of considerable size, not covered in our study.

In connection with indirect CMEA capital holdings, mention must also be made of Austrian companies belonging to the Communist Party of Austria (KPÖ-Konzern). This group of firms presently comprises about fifty companies with an estimated turnover of Sch.5 – 10,000m, most of which belong to twenty trustees of the Communist Party of Austria (KPÖ).[7] In many cases, an intermediate role is played by Swiss and Liechtenstein trustees and holding companies. The KPÖ-Konzern largely came into being during the Soviet occupation of Austria (1945–55), and for years it had a virtual monopoly of trade between Austria and Eastern Europe. The enterprises of the KPÖ-Konzern are to be viewed as Austrian enterprises whose business purpose is solely to finance the Austrian Communist Party through their profits;[8] they are therefore not included in this study. In a number of cases, however, capital ownership is 'mixed': both the CMEA countries and the Austrian Communist Party have holdings. The Austrian Communist Party capital ownership has been classified as an Austrian capital holding; however, it is possible that in some cases a trust exists whose beneficiary is not the Austrian Communist Party but the CMEA country concerned.

The empirical basis of the study

The study is based on an investigation of enterprises with CMEA capital holdings listed in Austrian trade registers; the information obtained reflects the situation at the end of October 1982 and was supplemented by research abroad, as well as by information from other sources (including the Chamber of Labour) and press reports. In the few cases of *Aktiengesellschaften*, their published balances provided relatively comprehensive data. Only in some cases was it possible to obtain information on the number of employees and the turnover of the CMEA firms.

An investigation into foreign direct investments in Austria, carried out by the Oesterreichische Nationalbank (OeNB, Austrian National Bank), which we refer to here as the OeNB investigation, represented both an important addition to and a check on this material. The Austrian National Bank kindly made this information on CMEA firms in Austria available to us. Statistics on Austria's regional balance of payments (CMEA direct investments) as well as on the regional status of Austrian credit institutions (CMEA capital holdings) were also evaluated.

Empirical results of the study

It was possible to identify a total of sixty firms, that is, enterprises which were CMEA owned or in which the CMEA countries have direct or indirect holdings in Austria.[9] Six of these enterprises are agencies of transport firms owned by the CMEA countries.

Table 5.1 *Number and capital of Austrian firms in which CMEA countries participate, 1982*

	Firms		Capital*	
	(no.)	(%)	(Sch. m.)	(%)
Hungary	23	38.4	97.79	14.3
Poland	9	15.0	186.91	27.3
Czechoslovakia	5	8.3	19.06	2.8
GDR	6	10.0	5.39	0.8
Bulgaria	6	10.0	3.08	0.4
Romania	3	5.0	1.02	0.1
Total, excluding Soviet Union	52	86.7	313.25	45.8
Soviet Union	8	13.3	371.20	54.2
Total, East Europe	60	100.0	684.45	100.0

* Total, i.e. including shares held by firms from Austria and third countries.

By far the largest number of CMEA firms belongs to Hungary (twenty-three firms, or 38.4 per cent of the total), followed by Poland (nine firms, or 15 per cent), the Soviet Union (eight firms), the GDR and Bulgaria (six firms each), Czechoslovakia (five firms), and Romania (three firms). No enterprises were discovered in which two or more CMEA countries had holdings at the same time (see Table 5.1).

The total capital of the Socialist companies amounts to Sch.684.5m, of which Sch.473.5m (69.2 per cent) is directly owned and a further Sch.54.6m (7.9 per cent) is indirectly owned by the CMEA countries (see Table 5.2). This indirect capital ownership is largely the capital of foreign enterprises belonging to the CMEA countries and having holdings in Austrian firms; a comparatively small role is played by indirect capital ownership through holdings in Austrian enterprises. Of the total capital of these firms, Sch.69.2m, or 10.1 per cent, is owned by Austrian firms or individuals; Sch.87.2m (12.7 per cent) is owned by firms or individuals from third countries. The capital holdings of third countries in companies with CMEA participation largely result from one particular case, the Centro-Bank, a joint foundation of Polish, Austrian, English, Italian, and French banks, registered in Vienna.

Enterprises in which the Soviet Union has holdings account for 54.2 per cent (Sch.371m) of the total capital of CMEA firms in

Table 5.2 *Relative proportions of capital held in Austrian firms in which CMEA countries participate, 1982*

	Direct CMEA participation	Indirect CMEA participation		Austrian participation	Third country participation	Total	Country share of direct CMEA participation (%)
		via Austria	via third countries				
1. Value (sm)							
Hungary	69.19	0.35	25.24	2.74	0.28	97.80	14.6
Poland	44.48	—	0.11	57.33	85.00	186.91	9.4
Czechoslovakia	0.04	—	14.04	3.11	1.88	19.06	0.0
GDR	3.24	0.60	—	2.08	0.07	5.39	0.7
Bulgaria	2.42	—	—	.06	—	3.08	0.5
Romania	0.22	—	0.28	0.52	—	1.02	0.0
Total, excluding Soviet Union	119.58	0.95	39.66	65.84	87.22	313.25	25.2
Soviet Union	353.88	—	14.00	3.32	—	371.20	74.7
Total. CMEA	473.46	0.95	53.66	69.16	87.22	684.45	100.0
2. Shares in each category							
Hungary	70.8	0.4	25.8	2.8	0.3	100.0	—
Poland	23.8	—	0.1	30.7	45.5	100.0	—
Czechoslovakia	0.2	—	73.7	16.3	9.8	100.0	—
GDR	60.0	—	—	38.6	1.3	100.0	—
Bulgaria	78.7	19.5	—	1.8	—	100.0	—
Romania	21.6	—	27.5	51.0	—	100.0	—
Total, excluding Soviet Union	38.2	0.3	12.7	21.0	27.8	100.0	—
Soviet Union	95.3	0.0	3.8	0.9	—	100.0	—
Total CMEA	69.2	0.1	7.8	10.1	12.7	100.0	

Table 5.3 *Austrian firms with participation by CMEA countries: share of capital directly owned by CMEA countries participating in Austrian firms, 1982*

	100%	*	50–99%	Under 50%	Total
		Number of firms in range:			
Hungary	8	(2)	6	9	23
Poland	1	(1)	5	3	9
Czechoslovakia	2	(2)	0	3	5
GDR	1	(1)	4	1	6
Bulgaria	2	(1)	2	2	6
Romania	2	(1)	0	1	3
Total, excluding the					
Soviet Union	16	(8)	17	19	52
As percentage	30.8	(15.3)	32.7	36.5	100.0
Soviet Union	5	(3)	3	0	8
As percentage	62.5	(37.5)	37.5	0.0	100.0
Total, CMEA	21	(11)	20	19	60
As percentage	35.0	(18.3)	33.3	31.7	100.0

* Where share is 100%, the number of these represented by agencies.

Austria; enterprises in which Poland has a holding account for 27.3 per cent (Sch.186.9m); enterprises in which Hungary has a holding account for 14.3 per cent; and enterprises in which Czechoslovakia has a holding account for 2.8 per cent of the total. However, if we calculate the individual CMEA countries' shares in capital which is directly owned by CMEA countries (Sch.473.5m), we reach a different result: by far the largest share (74.7 per cent) is owned by the Soviet Union, a further 14.6 per cent by Hungary, and only 9.4 per cent by Poland (see last column, Table 5.2).

Judging by the direct capital ownership of the CMEA states, only twenty-one enterprises (35 per cent) are 100 per cent CMEA owned.[10] In a further twenty enterprises (33.3 per cent) over half the capital is CMEA owned, while in nineteen cases (31.7 per cent), direct CMEA capital ownership accounts for less than half the enterprise capital. The Soviet Union either has a majority interest or owns 100 per cent of the capital in all the firms in which it participates in Austria (see Table 5.3).

The legal form preferred by the CMEA states is that of the *GesmbH* (thirty-seven cases out of fifty-three cases for which the legal form

Table 5.4 *Legal forms of Austrian firms with CMEA participation, 1982*

	Aktienge-sellschaften	GesmbH	GesmbH und Co. Kommandit-sellschaften	Agencies	Total
No of firms					
Hungary	2	16	2	1	21
Poland	1	6	1	0	8
Czechoslovakia	1	2	0	2	5
GDR	0	4	1	—	5
Bulgaria	0	4	0	1	5
Romania	0	2	0	—	2
Total, excluding Soviet Union	4	34	4	4	46
Soviet Union	2	3	0	2	7
Total, CMEA	6	37	4	6	53
Share (%)					
Total, excluding Soviet Union	9.3	79.1	9.3	9.3	100.0
Soviet Union	28.5	42.9	0.0	28.5	100.0
Total, CMEA	11.3	69.8	7.5	11.3	100.0
Company capital (Sch. m)					
Total, excluding Soviet Union	208.0	103.29	1.96	—	313.25
Soviet Union	360.0	11.2	0	—	371.2
Total, CMEA	568.0	114.49	1.96	—	684.45
Share of company capital (%)					
Total, excluding Soviet Union	66.4	33.0	0.7	—	100.0
Soviet Union	97.0	3.0	0.0	—	100.0
Total, CMEA	83.0	16.7	0.3	—	100.0
Average company capital/firm (Sch. m)					
Total, excluding Soviet Union	52.0	3.04	0.18	—	7.46*
Soviet Union	180.0	3.73	—	—	74.24*
Total, CMEA	94.7	3.09	0.18	—	14.56*

* Excluding agencies.

could be identified or 70 per cent of the total). The preference for this company form is probably to be explained by the following considerations:[11]

— the right to issue instructions to the managing director of a *GesmbH*;
— the fact that until the end of 1980, *GesmbHs* were not required by law to publish an annual report showing balances and the profit and loss account; since the law on *GesembHs* was amended, they have been required to publish such information to a limited extent;
— the fact that a *GesmbH* can be founded with a low capital outlay (a minimum capital of Sch.250,000 has been required to found a *GesmbH* since 1981).

A further four companies have the form of the *GesmbH und Co. KG* described earlier. Only six companies are *Aktiengesellschaften* (public limited companies); of these, four are banks or insurance companies, which in general are required to have this form, and the remaining two are industrial plants.

The *Aktiengesellschaften* account for the greater part of total CMEA enterprise capital (Sch.568m, or 83 per cent, while *GesmbHs* account for only Sch.114.5m (16.7 per cent).

Table 5.5   *CMEA participation in Austrian firms with capital of less than Sch. 1m, 1982*

| | Number of firms | Total capital (Sch. m) | Direct CMEA holdings (Sch. m) | Indirect CMEA participation | | Austrian capital (Sch. m) | Capital from third countries (Sch. m) |
				via Austria (Sch. m)	via third countries (Sch. m)		
Hungary	13	4.75	2.5675	0.35	0.435	1.3725	0.025
Poland	3	1.1	0.594	—	0.105	0.401	—
Czechoslovakia	2	1.06	0.04	—	0.9	—	0.12
GDR	3	1.228	0.875	—	—	0.282	0.071
Bulgaria	3	0.75	0.1	0.6	—	0.05	—
Romania	2	1.02	0.22	—	0.28	0.52	—
Total	26	9.908	4.3965	0.95	1.72	2.6255	0.216

Table 5.6   *Number of firms by registered location and year of foundation for Austrian firms with CMEA participation*

	Registered location		Year of foundation				
	Vienna	*Other*	*Up to 1944 (old holdings)*	*1945–70*	*Since 1971*	*Unknown*	*Total*
Hungary	20	3	3	5	11	4	23
Poland	9	0	—	4	3	2	9
Czechoslovakia	5	0	2	—	—	3	5
GDR	5	1	—	1	1	4	6
Bulgaria	6	0	1	2	1	2	6
Romania	3	0	—	—	—	3	3
Total, excluding Soviet Union	48	4	6	12	16	18	52
Soviet Union	8	0	—	1	4	3	8
Total, CMEA	56	4	6	13	20	21	60
as percentage	93.3	6.7	10.0	21.6	33.3	35.0	100.0

The average capital of individual CMEA enterprises (excluding agencies) in Austria amounts to Sch.15m. The average capital of individual *Aktiengesellschaften* amounts to Sch.94.7m (in the case of *Aktiengesellschaften* with Soviet participation, the average capital is Sch.180m; the remaining *Aktiengesellschaften* with CMEA participation have an average capital of Sch.52m). In contrast, the *GesmbHs* with CMEA participation have an average capital of only Sch.3.1m (see Table 5.4).

Almost half (twenty-six) of all Eastern European (excluding the Soviet Union) firms possess less than Sch.1m capital; 50 per cent of these small enterprises are owned by Hungary (see Table 5.5).

The great majority of enterprises in Austria with CMEA participation are registered in Vienna (see Table 5.6). Out of the total of sixty of CMEA firms, six are 'old holdings' that is, they were founded before the Second World War. A further thirteen firms were founded in the period 1945 – 70. The 1970s, when twenty firms were founded, was the period of the most intense activity. It was not possible to ascertain the year of foundation in twenty-one cases. The most recent founding of a firm on which information was available was in 1978. According to newspaper reports, there were some new cases of direct investment of CMEA countries in Austria in the last two or three years. At the end of 1982 the Austrian construction company Hoffmann und Maculan and the Hungarian foreign trade organization Emex-Export agreed to found a joint company in Vienna (the Austrian capital share is 51 per cent). The company is to participate in construction projects in the Near East and North Africa. In 1984 a joint firm, BERMA Industrieanlagen und Maschinenhandelsgesellschaft, was founded in Vienna by Mineralkontor, Vienna (51 per cent shareholding) and Technoimpex, Budapest (49 per cent). In 1985 the Austrian enterprise Winter Medizinaltechnik, and LABORMIN, Hungary, founded a joint venture for the production and marketing of *Katastrofencontainer*, a Hungarian development. In the spring of 1985 a Bulgarian enterprise group bought the Neunkirchener Schraubenwerk GmbH, employing 170 persons, for Sch.19m, a firm which had had to enter settlement proceedings.[12]

Austria's regional balance of payments statistics reveal the following direct investments in the non-banking sectors in Austria: Hungary Sch.2m in 1979, Sch.6m in 1980, and Sch.2n in 1981; Poland Sch.1m in 1980, Czechoslovakia Sch.7m in 1981; and the Soviet Union Sch.7m in 1983. There was a small amount of investment in the banking sector as well. These transactions probably resulted from additions to capital or participation in already existing firms.

However, the CMEA countries' growing balance of payments problems may have prevented the foundation of more new CMEA firms in recent years. On the other hand, the possibility cannot be ruled out that, at least in some cases, the CMEA countries have secured an interest in existing enterprises, although we found little evidence of such investments.

So far as sectoral distribution is concerned, the situation is as follows: twenty-six firms, or 43.3 per cent of the total, are active in the field of trade. Five of the CMEA firms (four Hungarian and one Czechoslovakian) are industrial enterprises. A further four companies are banks and insurance companies, which together account for 83.0 per cent of total CMEA capital in Austria. Six enterprises are concerned with transport and freight; their average capital is double that of any of the trading firms. Another seven firms must be classified as 'Other'; in general, these are smaller companies with average capital of less than Sch.1m. Twelve CMEA firms are Eastern European transportation agencies, such as airlines (see Table 5.7).

Table 5.7 *Sectoral distribution of Austrian firms with CMEA participation, 1982**

		Trade	Industry	Banking, insurance	Transport, freight	Other	Subtotal	Transport agencies	Total
Hungary	Number	10 (6)	4 (1)	1 (1)	3 (1)	2 (2)	20 (11)	3 (3)	23 (14)
	Capital (Sch. m)	8.45	36.6	40.0	11.1	1.645	97.795	—	—
	Av. cap (Sch. m)	0.845	9.15	40.0	3.7	0.823	4.890		
Poland	Number	6 (4)	—	1 (0)	—	1 (1)	8 (5)	1 (1)	9 (6)
	Capital (Sch. m)	17.412	—	168.0	—	1.5	186.912	—	—
	Av. cap (Sch. m)	2.902	—	168.0	—	1.5	37.38		
Czechoslovakia	Number	1 (0)	1 (0)	—	—	1 (0)	3 (0)	2 (2)	5 (2)
	Capital (Sch. m)	0.9	18.0	—	—	0.16	19.06		
GDR	Number	4 (4)	—	—	—	1 (0)	5 (4)	1 (1)	6 (5)
	Capital (Sch. m)	5.288	—	—	—	1.1	5.388		
	Av. cap (Sch. m)	1.322							
Bulgaria	Number	3 (1)	—	—	2 (1)	—	5 (2)	1 (1)	6 (3)
	Capital (Sch. m)	0.75	—	—	2.325	—	3.075		
Romania	Number	1 (0)	—	—	—	1 (1)	2 (1)	1 (1)	3 (2)
	Capital (Sch. m)	0.8	—	—	—	0.22	1.02		
Total, excluding Soviet Union	Number	25 (15)	5 (1)	2 (1)	5 (2)	6 (4)	42 (23)	9 (9)	51 (32)
	Capital (Sch. m)	33.6	54.6	208.0	13.425	3.625	313.25		
	Av. cap (Sch. m)	1.344	10.92	104.0	3.356	0.604	7.458		
Soviet Union	Number	1 (1)	—	2 (2)	1 (1)	1 (1)	5 (5)	3 (3)	8 (8)
	Capital (Sch. m)	6.2	—	360.0	2.0	3.0	341.2		
	Av. cap (Sch. m)	6.2	—	180.0	2.0	3.0	74.24		

Table 5.7 continued

Total CMEA	26 (16)	5 (1)	4 (3)	6 (3)	7 (5)	48 (28)	12 (12)	60 (40)
Number	26 (16)	5 (1)	4 (3)	6 (3)	7 (5)	48 (28)	12 (12)	60 (40)
Capital (Sch. m)	39.8	54.6	568.0	15.425	6.625	684.45		
Av. cap (Sch. m)	1.531	10.92	142.0	3.085	0.946	14.562		
Distribution (%)								
Hungary	43.4	17.4	4.3	13.0	8.7	87.0	13.0	100.0
Poland	66.7	0.0	11.1	0.0	11.1	88.9	11.1	100.0
Total, excluding								
Soviet Union	48.1	9.6	3.8	9.6	11.5	82.6	17.3	100.0
Soviet Union	12.5	—	25.0	12.5	12.5	62.5	37.5	100.0
Total, CMEA	43.3	8.3	6.7	10.0	11.7	80.9	20.0	100.0
Company capital: share (%)								
Hungary	8.6	37.4	40.9	11.4	1.7	100.0	—	—
Poland	9.3	—	89.8	—	0.8	100.0	—	—
Total, excluding								
Soviet Union	10.7	17.4	66.4	4.3	1.2	100.0	—	—
Soviet Union	1.7	—	97.0	0.5	0.8	100.0	—	—
Total, CMEA	5.8	8.0	83.0	2.3	1.0	100.0	—	—

* The figures in brackets show the number of firms with over 50 per cent direct ownership by CMEA states.

Motives for and features of capital investments made by the CMEA states in Austria

In general, capital investments in foreign countries are rarely made for only one reason but, rather, usually have a number of more or less important motives behind them. This is also true of capital investments made by CMEA states in Austria. Our study has indicated that economic motives may well predominate. Motives other than economic may also play a role, but it is not possible to determine these with the instruments of economic research.

'Old holdings' left over from the time of Austro-Hungarian monarchy and the period between the two World Wars represent a special category of capital investment by the CMEA countries in Austria. In view of the close economic relations that existed between Austria and the countries which succeeded the Austro-Hungarian monarchy, the six companies which represent old holdings are really quite a small number. It is conceivable that, in the early post-war period, the Eastern European countries liquidated their capital investments in Austria and never renewed them.

The two larger industrial firms Tungsram,[13] with Hungarian ownership, and Koh-i-Noor Hardmuth, which is partly owned by Czechoslovakia,[14] are among the old holdings. Others are the Hungarian Central- und Wechselkreditbank[15] and the Czech firm Topham & Co.[16] The light-bulb factory Patria, a subsidiary of the Austrian Tungsram company, is also among the old holdings.

On the basis of the branch structure, it can be assumed that the CMEA companies based in Austria primarily serve to promote East–West trade. In addition, banks and freight companies take advantage of the opportunities in the service sector. The remaining CMEA enterprises engage in a wide range of activities, and it is unlikely that there is a unified concept behind these activities.

Just under half of all CMEA enterprises are trading firms. These enterprises also handle exports from Austria (and in some cases transit trade also), but their main task consists of selling and marketing products from their respective country of origin in Austria. In addition to this, these enterprises also serve the purpose of familiarizing CMEA foreign trade specialists with Western business practices and customs.

It was not possible to get a clear picture of the relationship between the CMEA firms and the enterprises of the KPÖ-Konzern. The fact that Austrian Communist Party (KPÖ) trustees participate in a number of CMEA firms would tend to support the conclusion that there is fairly close cooperation. On the other hand, the motivation of the two groups is probably different: in the case of the KPÖ-Konzern profits are most important, while by contrast the CMEA countries are interested in maximizing turnover and — in order to avoid Austrian profit taxes — in not making too much profit. The fact that the number of KPÖ-Konzern enterprises dropped from one hundred to fifty during the 1970s while the CMEA states founded an especially large number of trading companies in Austria seems to indicate that there is some competition between the two groups.

Generally the trading companies concerned are fairly small, with an average capital of Sch.1.5m per company. In most of the trading companies (sixteen out of twenty-six) the CMEA companies command a qualified majority of the capital (over 50 per cent).

Hungary owns the largest number of trading companies in Austria (ten). This is probably connected with the fact that Austria and Hungary have a common border and relatively intensive economic relations, but could also possibly be explained by economic reform, which has made more progress in Hungary than in other Eastern European countries. This reform has included an attempt to give the manufacturing enterprises a direct interest in exporting their goods. Most Hungarian trade enterprises in Austria conduct trade in finished industrial goods and foodstuffs.

Poland has an interest in six trading enterprises located in Austria. In contrast to the other CMEA countries, most of the Polish-owned companies were founded before 1970. The most important firm is Polcarbon, in which Poland holds a majority, and the Austrian Communist Party a minority, interest. This enterprise, which markets Polish coal and fuel oil in Austria, was already in existence in 1947. The Polish export company Dal, which began founding foreign subsidiaries immediately after the Second World War and holds more interests in Western countries than any other CMEA foreign trade organization,[17] has an interest in two Austrian business firms.

It is surprising that Czechoslovakia only holds an interest in one trading company (Topham & Co., an old holding). This might be attributable to the great reserve Czechoslovakia has shown towards cooperation with the West ever since the 1968 Soviet invasion. However, it is also conceivable that Czechoslovakia participates in Austrian business enterprises through trustees so that its participation is not identifiable, or that it continues to cooperate with the KPÖ-Konzern.

The German Democratic Republic has an interest in four trading enterprises,[18] whose primary purpose is marketing finished goods (machinery, and photographic articles) in Austria. Bulgaria participates in some smaller Austrian businesses (agricultural commodities, handicrafts), and the Soviet Union and Romania in one business enterprise each.

As far as CMEA industrial enterprises in Austria are concerned, most of these are old holdings (Tungsram, Patria, or Koh-i-Noor). Two other industrial enterprises under Hungarian ownership are of interest. One is a pharmaceutical concern, Enzypharm, which was already in existence in 1948 and in which Medimpex of Budapest participates. The other, Metex, belongs to the steel-working industry; its capital is provided by two holding companies in Liechtenstein. Metex may be an example of Hungarian plans to buy up Western firms that are in financial difficulties but can be restored to financial soundness.

In Austria the CMEA states participate in three banks and one insurance company. The Hungarian Central- und Wechselkredit-bank AG was founded many years ago, in 1918, and all Sch.40m of its share capital are in Hungarian ownership. The Centralbank handles all banking transactions. The Polish Centro Internationale Handels-bank AG (Centrobank) was founded as an *Aktiengesellschaft* in 1973 by transformation from the Centrofin-Finanzierungsgesell-schaft mbH, which had been established in 1971. The Centrobank's share capital amounts to Sch.178m, with the Polish Bank Handlowy holding Sch.32.5m of this capital and Austria's Bawag Sch.50.5m. The remaining capital is in the hands of English, French, and Italian banks. The Centrobank specializes in financing East–West trade, compensation transactions, and related activities. At the end of 1984 the ownership of the Centrobank was changed. The owners each with a share of 25 per cent are now the Genossenschaftliche Zentralbank, Austria; Bank Handlowy, Poland; Kleinworth Benson, Great Britain; and Banco di Sicilia, Italy. A Polish and an Austrian citizen make up the bank's managing board, while the head of the supervisory board (*Aufsichtsrat*) is Polish. In 1980 the Centrobank's balance sheet total amounted to Sch.4,400m.

As early as 1958 the Soviet Union had already founded the Garant-Versicherungs AG. This was one of the first important firms ever founded by the Soviet Union in a Western industrial nation after the Second World War. In 1974 the Soviet Union also established the Donaubank.

Four Soviet banks and foreign trade organizations hold a total of Sch.76m worth of the Garant AG's Sch.90m of share capital. The other shareholders are the Soviet-owned firms, the Black Sea and Baltic General Insurance Company of London and the Schwarzmeer-und Ostee Versicherungs AG of Hamburg, with a Sch.7m share-holding each. The Garant AG specializes in insurance connected with East–West trade, but is also involved in other types of insurance business and in addition handles reinsurance transactions. In 1980 the Garant AG collected Sch.81.6m in premiums and had a balance sheet total of Sch.363.4m. Both managing board directors are Soviet citizens.

The Donaubank's share capital of Sch.270m is divided between the State Bank of the Soviet Union (Sch.162m) and the Bank for Foreign Trade of the Soviet Union (Sch.108m). It specializes in financing East–West trade and handling related payment transactions. In 1980 the balance sheet total of the Donaubank was Sch.4,600m, and it had a staff of forty. Both managing board directors and also some of the directors and authorized signatories are Soviet citizens.

One important source of foreign currency for the CMEA states is their earnings from the transport and freight business. The CMEA firms operating in Austria in this area are not only interested in transporting goods as part of the bilateral trade between Austria and the CMEA states, but also in transit traffic between Western Europe and the Middle East. Bulgaria in particular has made special efforts to gain a share of the North–South transit business. It has an interest in one or two Austrian transport companies and is said to have twenty lorries registered in Austria.[19] The Hungarian firm Hungaro-camion of Vienna owns a freight business, and another Hungarian firm, Volan-Trust, holds an interest in a transport company in Bregenz. In 1976 the Soviet Union founded the freight agency Asotra in Vienna, in which Austrian freight agencies also participate.

In addition, the CMEA countries own seven other businesses in Austria. These include a Hungarian restaurant, a Polish consulting agency which also places Polish fitters, a Soviet convention-planning organization, and a branch of the Hungarian travel agency Ibusz. On the other hand, the Studio neuzeitlicher Ausbildung in Traun, in which the German Democratic Republic and the Federal Republic of Germany participate, does not appear to be a true business firm.

Table 5.8 *Dependence of the Austrian economy on foreign capital: overall and CMEA countries, 1979 and 1981*

	Overall*		Industry 1979	Services† 1979	Industry 1981	Services† 1981
	1979	1981				
1. Direct dependence on foreign countries						
Number of *firms* under foreign influence‡	1,701	1,754	636	1,065	631	1,123
Number of *employees* (in 1,000s)						
Austria total	2,070	2,056	621	1,449	605	1,451
under foreign influence	267	247	177	90	160	87
as % of all employees	13	12	29	6	26	6
2. Indirect dependence on foreign countries§						
Number of *firms* under foreign influence	720	721	328	392	314	407
Number of *employees* under foreign influence (1,000s)	94	104	44	50	43	61
as % of all employees	5	5	7	3	7	4
3. Nominal capital¶ of firms under direct foreign influence						
Total (Sch. m)	39,535	41,583	22,678	16,857	22,530	19,053

Table 5.8 *continued*

Of this, from: Austria	11,567	9,955	6,908	4,659	5,494	4,461
Foreign countries	27,968	31,628	15,770	12,198	17,030	14,592
CMEA countries**	405	528	102	303	17	511
as % ***	1.0	1.3	0.4	1.8	0.1	2.7
Soviet Union	162.0	—	—	—	—	—
Hungary	117.0	—	—	—	—	—
Czechoslovakia	88.2	—	—	—	—	—
Poland	35.9	—	—	—	—	—
GDR	2.0	—	—	—	—	—
By comparison: Switzerland, Liechtenstein	8,877	—	5,745	3,132	—	—
Federal Rep. of Germany	9,459	—	5,274	4,185	—	—
United States	3,160	—	1,655	1,505	—	—

* Agriculture and forestry as well as the civil service, which together employ 734,000 people, are not included.

† Including trades.

‡ Firms with nominal capital of at least S1m.

§ Holdings of firms under foreign influence in other Austrian firms.

¶ For *Kapitalgesellschaften* (joint-stock companies): share capital; for sole traderships and partnerships: assets of the owners in the capital accounts; for non-independent branch establishments: endowment funds or working capital.

** No data for Romania and Bulgaria.

*** Percentage of total nominal capital of firms under direct foreign influence.

Source: Oesterreichische Nationalbank (Austrian National Bank), *Mitteilungen des Direktoriums* (Board of Directors Report), No. 1 (1982) and No. 12 (1983). plus additional information from the OeNB.

The overall economic significance of CMEA capital holdings in Austria

Data collected by the Oesterreichische Nationalbank (OeNB) on direct investments made by foreign countries in Austria during the years 1979 and 1981[20] are a supplement to the information gained from the trade register and other sources about CMEA businesses in Austria. The OeNB study also makes it possible to gain an idea of the overall economic significance of these CMEA firms and permits a comparison of the two sources.

Direct foreign investments are considered to be foreign capital investments in Austrian firms which are made for the purpose of directly influencing the business activity of these firms.[21] In this connection three forms of direct investment can be distinguished: capital holdings, long-term credits, and reinvestment of profits. Portfolio investments are not included, since earnings are the main consideration in this type of investment.

According to the OeNB study, at the end of 1981 1,754 Austrian firms were subject to foreign influence due to direct foreign investments (see Table 5.8). However, only firms with a nominal capital of at least Sch.1m were included in the study. The OeNB estimates that, because of this limitation, about 20 to 30 per cent of total direct foreign investments in Austria were not taken into consideration; in the case of CMEA states, which participate primarily in smaller domestic firms, the share must certainly be greater.

The study also contained information about indirect foreign dependence. This comes into play when a firm which is under foreign influence participates in an Austrian firm. Altogether, direct foreign influence was found to exist in the case of 721 Austrian firms.

At the end of 1981, 247,000 people, or about 12 per cent of all employees, were employed in companies under direct foreign influence.[22] In the industrial sector 26 per cent of all employees worked in enterprises directly dependent on foreign capital, and in the services sector this proportion was 6 per cent. In addition, 5 per cent of Austrian workers were employed in Austrian firms indirectly under foreign influence (7 per cent of industrial and 4 per cent of service workers).

The nominal capital[23] of the enterprises under direct foreign influence amounted in 1981 to Sch.41,583m, of which Sch.22,530m was in the industrial sector and Sch.19,053m in the services sector. Of this capital, Sch.9.955m was Austrian and Sch.31,628m foreign.

According to the OeNB survey, the nominal capital belonging to the CMEA countries in 1981 amounted to Sch.528m, or 1.3 per cent of the total nominal capital under direct foreign influence. Of this amount, Sch.17m (0.1 per cent) was invested in industry and Sch.511m (2.7 per cent) in the service sector.

These percentages may also be used to calculate the total number of persons employed in CMEA-influenced firms, and the resulting figure is about 3,200 persons. If the smaller businesses (with nominal capital of less than Sch.1m) and the firms indirectly under foreign influence are included, the total number of workers in such CMEA firms can be estimated at about 5,000 to 6,000. According to the OeNB survey, in 1979 the Soviet Union had the largest amount of direct investments (Sch.162m), followed by Hungary (Sch.117m), Czechoslovakia (Sch.88m), and Poland (Sch.36m) out of a total of Sch.405m for all CMEA countries (a breakdown by countries is not available for 1981).

Comparison of the Trade-Register and OeNB Studies

The OeNB estimates that East European investments amounted to a nominal capital of Sch.405m in 1979, which was about 65m or (14 per cent) less than the trade-register figure of 469m as the value of direct CMEA capital holdings in Austria.[24] (see Table 5.9). This difference occurs mainly because of different closing dates for these statistical surveys, but in part it is also due to a different concept of nominal capital. A country-by-country comparison shows that Czechoslovakia clearly participates in one or more enterprises (nominal capital 88m) which are not included in the trade-register data.

According to the regional status of Austrian credit institutions, at the end of 1983 the CMEA states held the following long-term interests in Austrian banks: Poland — Sch.39m; Hungary — Sch.100m; and the Soviet Union — Sch.270m. According to the trade-register statistics, direct CMEA capital holdings in Austrian banks in 1982 were as follows: the Polish Centrobank — Sch.33m; the Hungarian Centrobank — Sch.40m; and the Soviet Donaubank — Sch.270m. The reason for the difference in the size of the sum quoted for Hungary could not be determined.

Table 5.9   *Trade-register and OeNB study of Austrian firms with CMEA participation: a comparison*

	No. of firms	Trade-register study* Directly-owned company capital			OeNB study ‡
		Total	Large firms (Sch. m)	Small firms †	Nominal capital (Sch. m)
Hungary	23	69.2	66.6	2.6	117.0
Poland	9	44.5	43.9	0.6	35.9
Czechoslovakia	5	0.0	0.0	0.0	88.2
GDR	6	3.2	2.3	0.9	2.0
Bulgaria	6	2.4	2.3	0.1	—
Romania	3	0.2	0.0	0.2	—
Total, excluding Soviet Union	52	119.6	115.2	4.4	243.0
Soviet Union	8	353.9	353.9	0.0	162.0
Total, CMEA	60	473.5	469.1	4.4	405.0

* 1982
† Company capital less than Sch. 1m.
‡ 1979 and 1982

Comparison with other studies

Up to now data about direct investments by CMEA states in Austria had only been collected once before, during the course of an international study at Carleton University in Canada[25], which Professor Carl McMillan has dealt with in various publications. The basis for the data in the Carleton *Directory* was published reports and a survey which built upon them. The 1978 edition of the *Directory* includes data about thirty-three CMEA firms in Austria. Our study does not include three of the firms listed in the *Directory* (see Table 5.10).[26] The trade register lists sixty firms; however, twelve of these are agencies which were not included in the *Directory*. If we use fully comparable data, the present study contains about nineteen more firms than the *Directory*. In particular, more Hungarian (seven) and GDR (four) firms were included. The larger number of CMEA firms in our study is probably not due to the fact that it was made a few years after the *Directory* was compiled: as already pointed out, none of the CMEA firms in our study was founded after 1979. However, it is possible that in some cases CMEA states acquired already existing Austrian firms after 1979.

Table 5.10 *Comparison of trade-register study with other studies on Number of Austrian firms with CMEA participation*

| | Carleton Directory[1] Nov. 1977 | Carleton Directory[2] End of 1978 | Trade-register study | | |
			Total	Excluding agencies	Difference*
Hungary	13	14†	23	21	+8‡
Poland	4	7	9	8	+1
Czechoslovakia	0	1	5	3	+2
GDR	3	3†	6	5	+3‡
Bulgaria	2	2	6	5	+3
Romania	2	2†	3	2	+1‡
Total, excluding Soviet Union	24	29¶	52	44	+18‡
Soviet Union	3	4	8	5	+1
Total, CMEA	27	33	60	49	+19‡

* Difference between trade-register study (excluding agencies) and McMillan(2).
† Includes one firm not listed in the trade-register study.
‡ Taking into account the difference explained in note 1 on p. 129.
¶ Includes three firms not listed in the trade-register study.

Sources: 1 C.H. McMillan, *Direct Soviet and East European Investment in the Industrialized Western Economies*, Working Paper No. 7, East–West Commercial Relations Series, Institute of Soviet and East European Studies, Carleton University, Ottawa, 1978.
2 C.H. McMillan, 'Growth of External Investments by the Comecon Countries', *The World Economy*, **2**, No. 3 (September 1979), based on *Directory of Soviet and East European Companies in the West*, East–West Project, Carleton University.

Notes

1. F. Levcik and J. Stankovsky, *Industrial Cooperation Between East and West*, London, MacMillan, 1979.
2. F. Levcik and J. Stankovsky, '*Recent Trends in Tripartite Industrial Cooperation: Austria's Experience*', study for UNCTAD, Geneva, 1978.
3. With the exception of the mixed form, *Gesellschaft mit beschränkter Haftung und Co. KG* (see comments on this form later in the chapter), as well as of the non-independent branch establishments of CMEA firms.
4. In the classification according to sectors, these cases appear together in the separate category of transportation agencies.

5. See the description of interrelations with the KPÖ Konzern in the following pages.
6. The following are thought to be some of the holding companies for Hungary: Centropa-Handels AG, Bern; Bernard-Trust, Vaduz; Metimexco, Vaduz; Stahlcometall, Mauren; and for Czechoslovakia: Save, Geneva; Arrow, Lugano.
7. In 1982 a good deal of public attention was attracted by legal proceedings in which the owner of a large petroleum trading firm (Turmöl) contested the existence of a trusteeship to the benefit of the Communist Party of Austria (KPÖ) and claimed the firm as his sole property. During the course of these proceedings many interesting details about the origin and interlocking relations of the KPÖ-Konzern became known. See Peter Muzik and Michael Schano, Die linken Kapitalisten (The Capitalists of the Left), *Trend*, No. 3 (1981), pp. 66–90.
8. The Communist Party is very weak in Austria (about 16,000 members and 45,000 voters); membership dues, contributions, etc. only add up to about Sch.4m. Despite this the KPÖ has an extensive party apparatus with full-time workers, and spends large sums on public relations. It is estimated that the annual deficit of the low-circulation daily newspaper *Volksstimme* amounts to between Sch.30m and 50m.
9. In the case of two firms it was not possible to determine CMEA ownership with absolute certainty; the travel agency Phönix (Czechoslovakia) may have been sold, while the firm Polygraph is more likely to be part of the KPÖ-Konzern. Information about these firms is included in the tables, but they were not considered in the study.
10. In the case of agencies of CMEA firms in Austria for which the percentage of capital ownership was not known, it was also assumed that they are solely owned by the CMEA parent company.
11. See J. Peischer, 'Auslandseinfluss in der österreichischen Wirtschaft unverändert . . .' (Foreign Influence on Austrian Economy Unchanged . . .), *Information über multinationale Konzerne*, No. 2 (1982).
12. These new CMEA enterprises are not included in the statistics.
13. A manufacturer of light bulbs and chandeliers, founded in 1891. Tungsram has a share capital of Sch.30m, 360 employees, and a turnover of about Sch.120m.
14 A manufacturer of pencils and wholesale trader in writing materials, founded in 1790 Koh-i-Noor has a share capital of Sch.18m, 125 employees, and a turnover of about Sch.45m. Czechoslovakia does not participate in Koh-i-Noor directly but through the Swiss firm Save, which holds a majority interest.
15. Founded 1918; its share capital is Sch.40m.
16. Share capital Sch.0.9m, 30 employees. Directly owned by Czechoslovakia until 1975; since 1975 indirect ownership via two Swiss holding companies.
17. Carl H. McMillan, 'Growth of External Investments by the Comecon Countries', *The World Economy*, No.3 (September 1979). p. 381.
18. One firm as general partner (*Komplementär*) of a *Kommandirgesellschaft*.

19. E. Hoorn, 'Frächter aus dem Comecon haben Österreich erobert' (Comecon Freighters Conquer Austria) *Presse Wien*, 22 December 1982. The firm Vienna-Transport is probably also under Bulgarian ownership; however, this is not evident in the trade register, so that it seems likely that a trusteeship is involved.

20. 'Ausländische Direktinvestitionen in Österreich, Stand End 1979' (Direct Foreign Investments in Austria as of the End of 1979), *Mitteilungen des Direktoriums der Oesterreichischen Nationalbank*, No. 1 (1982), pp. 16–23; '. . . Ende 1981', No. 12 (1983) (see Table 5.8).

21. Foreign investments are officially defined as follows: 'Direct foreign investments are capital investments made by non-resident aliens within a country in order to establish or maintain lasting economic relations with a domestic firm, while at the same time there is an intention of influencing the business activity of the firm.' Ibid., 1982, p. 16.

22. Those working in agriculture and the public sector were not included in this calculation.

23. The following are considered nominal capital: for joint-stock companies (*Kapitalgesellschaften*) — share capital; for sole traderships and partnership — assets of the owners in the capital accounts; for non-independent branch establishments — endowment funds or working capital.

24. Excluding firms with less than Sch.1m capital, which are not included in the OeNB study.

25. R. Bruce Morgan and J. Reid Henry, *Directory of Soviet and East European Companies in the West*, Institute of Soviet and E. European Studies, Carleton University, Ottawa, 1979.

26. In 1977 the entry for AURO-Chemie GesmbH (Romania) was removed from the trade register; Gränges GesmbH (GDR) is probably completely owned by Sweden; the firm International Oil, Pharmaceutical and Chemical Equipment does not appear in any Austrian trade register.

6 Socialist multinationals in developing countries

Eugène Zaleski

Introduction

The lack of information on socialist multinationals in developing countries makes any survey of these organizations a difficult task. The data available from the CMEA countries themselves are far from complete, partly because some of the information on the activities of socialist multinationals is regarded as almost on a par with state secrets. Furthermore, as there are more than one hundred developing countries located on three different continents holding different views on the necessity of publishing economic data, it is not surprising that there is no standardized data base relating to the activities of the socialist multinationals in the Third World.

The first major surveys[1] on this theme were published some six years ago by Professor Carl McMillan of Carleton University, Ottawa, and research activity in this field has been maintained at Carleton as part of an ongoing research programme on East–West commercial activities. The research described in this chapter has attempted to update some of McMillan's earlier results and to carry out an independent survey in this field using mainly reviews and articles published by specialist journals available in France. Information was obtained on CMEA joint ventures (mixed enterprises) at various stages in their commercial development, namely:

(a) those which were already operating;
(b) those which were in the process of establishment;
(c) those for which an agreement to proceed to establishment had been made by the relevant authorities

We used McMillan's findings to a considerable extent, although we were not always able to identify some of the mixed enterprises which he mentions. From the comparative figures given in Table 6.1 it can be seen that McMillan's identification of the number of mixed enterprises exceeded this present survey's by a total of seventeen. This could be due to unavoidable incompleteness in both sets of data, since published reports do not always state the trading names of these companies accurately and since some of the multinationals have set up their own subsidiaries which are sometimes difficult to identify. In any event a 10 per cent difference in estimates of numbers (185 and 168 respectively) is probably no great cause for concern when we remember the possible sources of error in research such as this.

According to this present survey, Poland has ten, Czechoslovakia eight, and Bulgaria seven fewer mixed enterprises than those

Table 6.1 *A comparison of the number of CMEA joint ventures (mixed enterprises) in developing countries identified by McMillan* and by Zaleski*

Region	Bulgaria	Czecho-slovakia	GDR	Hungary	Poland	Romania	Soviet Union	Total
Africa†								
McMillan	12	4	—	6	16	31	8	75
Zaleski	6	5	—	5	10	30	14	70
Asia								
McMillan	4	4	1	8	8	2	7	34
Zaleski	5	2	1	10	6	2	7	33
Latin America								
McMillan	—	13	—	5	7	7	4	36
Zaleski	—	7	2	8	3	7	9	36
Middle East								
McMillan	5	3	—	12	5	9	6	40
Zaleski	3	2	—	9	5	6	4	29
Total‡								
McMillan	21	24	1¶	31	34	49	25	185
Zaleski	14	16	3	32	24	45	34	168

* 'Growth of External Investments by the Comecon Countries', pp. 363–86.

† Excluding Egypt, which is included in the Middle East area.

‡ According to the United Nations Conference on Trade and Development, there are now some one hundred socialist mixed enterprises in developing countries, but UNCTAD make the usual reservations about the completeness of these estimates. (*Ways and Means of Expanding Trade and Economic Relations between Countries Having Different Economic and Social Systems*, Study by UNCTAD Secretariat, TD/B/AC.38/2, 12 April 1982, p. 12).

Table 6.2   *Number and location of CMEA joint ventures (mixed enterprises) in developing countries, April 1984*

Region	Bulgaria	Czecho-slovakia	GDR	Hungary	Poland	Romania	Soviet Union	Total
Africa								
Angola	—	—	—	—	—	1	1	2
Benin	1	—	—	—	—	—	—	1
Burundi	—	—	—	—	—	2	—	2
Cameroon	—	—	—	—	—	—	1	1
Central African Republic	—	—	—	—	—	3	—	3
Congo (Brazzaville)	—	—	—	—	—	1	1	2
Ivory Coast	—	—	—	—	—	1	—	1
Ethiopia	—	—	—	—	—	—	1	1
Gabon	—	—	—	—	—	3	—	3
Ghana*	—	—	—	—	—	—	—	—
Guinea	—	—	—	—	—	1	1	2
Liberia	—	—	—	—	—	1	—	1
Libya	1	—	—	—	—	4	—	5
Madagascar	—	—	—	—	—	—	1	1
Mauritania	—	—	—	—	—	1	1	2
Morocco	1	1	—	—	2	3	2	9
Mozambique	—	—	—	1	—	—	2	3
Nigeria	3	2	—	4	7	3	1	20
Senegal	—	—	—	—	1	1	—	2
Sierra Leone	—	—	—	—	—	—	1	1
Somalia	—	—	—	—	—	—	1	1
Sudan†	—	—	—	—	—	—	—	—
Tanzania	—	—	—	—	—	1	—	1
Tunisia	—	1	—	—	—	—	—	1
Zaire	—	—	—	—	—	2	—	2
Zambia	—	1	—	—	—	1	—	2
Zimbabwe	—	—	—	—	—	1	—	1
Africa total	6	5	—	5	10	30	14	70
Asia								
Afghanistan	—	—	—	1	—	—	1	2
Bangladesh	—	—	—	1	—	—	—	1
India	2	1	1	5	4	1	1	15
Pakistan	—	—	—	2	—	—	—	2
Philippines	—	—	—	—	—	—	1	1
Singapore	3	1	—	—	2	—	3	9
Thailand	—	—	—	1	—	1	1	3
Asia total	5	2	1	10	6	2	7	33

Region	Bulgaria	Czecho-slovakia	GDR	Hungary	Poland	Romania	Soviet Union	Total
Latin America								
Argentina	—	1	—	1	1	—	1	4
Bermuda	—	—	—	—	—	1	—	1
Brazil	—	—	—	2	—	—	—	2
Chile	—	1	—	—	—	1	—	2
Costa Rica	—	—	—	—	—	—	1	1
El Salvador	—	—	—	—	—	—	1	1
Ecuador	—	—	—	—	—	—	1	1
Guyana	—	—	1	—	—	—	1	2
Mexico	—	4	1	—	—	1	1	7
Panama	—	—	—	1	—	1	—	2
Peru	—	1	—	3	2	2	1	9
Trinidad & Tobago	—	—	—	—	—	—	1	1
Venezuela	—	—	—	1	—	1	1	3
Latin America total	—	7	2	8	3	7	9	36
Middle East								
Dubai	—	—	—	1	—	—	—	1
Egypt	—	—	—	—	1	1	1	3
Iran	1	1	—	3	2	1	1	9
Kuwait	—	—	—	1	—	—	—	1
Lebanon	2	1	—	4	2	4	1	14
Iraq	—	—	—	—	—	—	1	1
Middle East total	3	2	—	9	5	6	4	29
Total, all regions	14	16	3	32	24	45	34	168

* One mixed enterprise with Cuban participation and one with Yugoslav participation.
† One mixed enterprise with Yugoslav participation.

identified by McMillan, whereas the Soviet Union has nine more. Africa is where the differences between the present survey and McMillan's are the most striking: McMillan identifies a larger number of Polish and Bulgarian mixed enterprises and a smaller number of Soviet enterprises. In the Middle East, McMillan counts a larger number of Bulgarian, Hungarian, Romanian, and Soviet mixed enterprises.

Geographical location, ownership, and commercial activities of socialist multinationals in the developing countries

Geographical location and ownership

Our survey shows that Africa is the preferred zone for CMEA countries to establish and develop mixed enterprises, since out of a total of 168, seventy were found to be located in that region compared with thirty-six in Latin America, thirty-three in Asia, and twenty-nine in the Middle East (see Table 6.2). The most important host country was found to be Nigeria, with twenty mixed enterprises, followed by India (fifteen enterprises), Lebanon (fourteen enterprises), and Morocco, Singapore, Peru, and Iran (nine enterprises each). There is clearly scope for further research on CMEA-owned mixed enterprises in these countries.

Romania has the largest number of enterprises located in developing countries (forty-five enterprises), followed by the Soviet Union (thirty-four enterprises), Hungary (thirty-two enterprises), and Poland (twenty-four enterprises). This result may be influenced by the publishing policy of Romania, however, as it is the only CMEA country which provides a list of its enterprises in the developing countries. As mentioned previously, information on the participation in ownership of the other CMEA countries was obtained through reports in newspapers and journals, and is therefore probably incomplete. There would seem to be a serious lack of data for the GDR, for example, since it does not appear to have any venture in Africa and very few in the other developing regions,[2] although the present author has been informed privately that it has a similar number of enterprises to Czechoslovakia in the developing countries. Nevertheless, Romania would appear to have a strong interest in Africa, with thirty of its forty-five reported enterprises located in that region and Romanian-African commercial activity consequently presents itself as a topic for further research. In addition, this present research has revealed a larger number of Soviet joint ventures than those reported by McMillan in 1979,[3] indicating that it would be useful to carry out a more detailed study of Soviet commercial activity through wholly-owned or partly-owned companies in the developing countries.

As part of this present survey's aim to extend previous research in this area, we have also sought data on the mixed enterprise activities

Table 6.3 *Number and location of Cuban and Yugoslav joint ventures (mixed enterprises) in developing countries, 1984*

Country and sector of activity	Cuba	Yugoslavia
Angola		
Resources development (including fishery)	1	
Prefabricated material	1	
School buildings	1	
Ghana		
Maize crop and animal husbandry		1
Sugar industry	1	
Libya		
Aluminium foundry		1
Natural resources	1	
Guinea		
Mining (bauxite and iron), forestry, fishery		3
Nigeria		
Building, agriculture, fishery		1
Sudan		
Construction and road maintenance		1
Zaire		
Maize in lower Zaire		1
Zambia		
Pepper, lead, zinc mining and processing		1
Mexico		
Oil company (Venezuela and Soviet Union)	1	
Peru		
Fishery	1	
Venezuela		
Oil company (Mexico and Soviet Union)	1	
Total	8	9

Table 6.4 *Distribution of CMEA joint ventures (mixed enterprises) in developing countries by activity, 1984*

Main activity	Bulgaria	Czecho-slovakia	GDR	Hungary	Poland	Romania	Soviet Union	Total
				(no. of enterprises)				
Trading	6	3	—	3	—	7	6	25
Production								
Manufacturing and assembling industry	3	3	1	13	3	4	—	27
Natural resources prospecting and development	—	—	—	—	—	10	4	14
Forestry and wood economics	—	—	—	—	—	6	—	6
Agricultural and food industry	—	—	—	—	—	9	2	11
Fisheries	—	—	—	—	2	2	3	7
Construction	1	—	—	3	—	1	4	9
Services								
General	1	—	—	—	—	—	—	1
Banking and Insurance	—	—	—	—	—	2	4	6
Transport	1	—	—	—	—	2	4	7
Activity unknown	2	10	2	13	19	2	7	55
Total	14	16	3	32	24	45	34	168

Note:UNCTAD (*Ways and Means of Expanding Trade and Economic Relations*, p.lc) provides the following data on the distribution of the one hundred socialist mixed enterprises in the developing countries: construction 15 per cent, equipment and machinery production and steel and iron industry 20 per cent, agriculture and forestry 15 per cent, mining industry and oil drilling 6 per cent, transfer of technology (machinery and design) 9 per cent, chemical industry 7 per cent, fisheries 6 per cent, transport 6 per cent.

of two other socialist countries which had not been studied previously, namely Cuba as an example of a non-European CMEA socialist member country and Yugoslavia as a European socialist country which does not belong to the CMEA. The data obtained for these countries are presented in Table 6.3, which reveals Cuba's preference for commercial activity in Angola. The incompleteness of the data makes it difficult to draw any substantial conclusion from this initial survey, but we consider it to be appropriate to take Cuba and Yugoslavia into account in any future research on socialist multinationals in the developing countries.

Sectors of activity

It can be seen from Table 6.4, which shows the results of the present survey classified according to the method followed by McMillan, that production was the main activity of sixty-five out of 113 (or 58 per cent) mixed enterprises with known activities. This was followed by trading (twenty-five out of the 113 mixed enterprises, or 22 per cent), construction (nine enterprises, or 8 per cent), transport (seven enterprises, or 6 per cent), and banking and insurance (six enterprises, or 5 per cent). It appears therefore, that trading or exporting activities are secondary to manufacturing for the majority of socialist multinationals in the developing countries. This conclusion would certainly not contradict the results presented in McMillan's 1979 paper,[4] and it also serves to contrast the activities of socialist multinationals in developing countries with those in Western Europe as presented elsewhere in this volume.

As part of the further study of these 113 enterprises with known activities, the data on assembly and minor production activities were separated from those on major production activities and reclassified with trading, as shown in Table 6.5. This reclassification suggests that thirty-nine (or 35 per cent) of the enterprises may be concerned with trading and allied minor production activities. Consequently, trading may not be such a secondary activity as was initially suggested by our original classification, and further research is indicated on this point. Table 6.5 also shows, however, that sixty mixed enterprises or 53 per cent, are concerned with production including research and engineering services (compared with 58 per cent in the 1979 McMillan survey).

Consequently, both surveys highlight production as the main activity of CMEA mixed enterprises in developing countries. Furthermore, it comes as no surprise to find that 25 per cent of these enterprises are concerned with developing natural resources (nine in fisheries and six in the wood industry). Only ten enterprises were found in the mining and energy sector (oil-extracting industries and coal and ore mining), but in these industries the number of enterprises is probably not as relevant as their size.

Table 6.5 *Economic activities of CMEA joint ventures (mixed enterprises) in developing countries, 1983*

Activity	No. of enterprises
1. Trading	
General*	15
Machinery (general)*	2
Machinery maintenance	1
Agricultural machinery	1
Lorries	1
Cars †	2
Tractors †	1
Petroleum products	1
Mineral fertilizers	1
Natural gum ‡	1
Agricultural products ‡	1
Medicines †	12
Total	39
2. Mining and energy industry	
Oil	2
Coal	1
Iron ore	2
Copper ore	3
Lead and zinc ore	1
Electrification	1
Total	10
Manufacturing industry	
Electrical engineering	1
Thermal equipment	1
Drilling equipment	1
Hydraulic equipment	1
Machine tools	1
Ball-bearings	1
Medical instruments	1
Cement	1
Mineral fertilizers	1
Leather	1
Flour milling	1
Fish processing	1
Chemical industry (albumine, globuline) biological products	1
Textiles	1
Total	14

Activity	No. of enterprises
4. Agricultural production	
Seeds and tree plantations	1
Industrial crop (cotton)	2
Breeding (sheep, poultry)	2
Agricultural processing	2
Soil improvement and irrigation	2
Total	9
5. Natural resources development	
Fisheries	9
Wood	6
Total	15
6. Prospecting	3
7. Construction	
General	6
Cartography and technical dsign	1
Engineering and consulting	2
Total	9
8. Transport	
General	2
Marine	4
Railway	1
Total	7
9. Banking and insurance	
Banking	5
Insurance	1
Total	6
10. Tourism	1
Total, all sectors	113

* Although these enterprises appear to be specialized, the nature of the specialization was not indicated.
† Assembly and trading,
‡ Trading and production.

It is also interesting to note that socialist multinationals' manufacturing industry spans a wide range of activities (equipment, machinery, and instruments manufacturing and chemicals, food, and textiles production) and that each of the fourteen identified mixed enterprises was found to carry out a different activity. In the agricultural sector, we found mainly animal-breeding, industrial crop, and agricultural processing activities, and although we identified only nine enterprises in this sector it is probable that many of those with non-identified activities were also concerned with agriculture. Transport and marine transport are also significant, essentially because of the activities of the Soviet merchant fleet.

Only five banks were located, four of which were entirely Soviet-owned (the Iranian-Soviet Bank and three subsidiaries of the Moscow Narodny Bank in Beirut and Singapore), and the Egyptian-Romanian Bank in Cairo, which has 49 per cent Romanian participation. These banks are important not in terms of numbers but in terms of capital investment and credit availability.

Capital investment

Data on the investments and assets of socialist mixed enterprises in developing countries proved to be so difficult to obtain that it was considered to be preferable to quote McMillan's figures on these topics and to extend them with our own data.

McMillan uses two kinds of estimates: (a) direct estimates for the mining and fishing industries and banking, and (b) analogies for other mixed enterprises. He attributes to the mixed enterprises located in developing countries the same average amount of assets as held by comparable mixed enterprises located in the OECD countries, obtaining an average value of assets per enterprise of $21m in the developing countries as against $15m in the OECD countries. This result is due to the larger part played by mining and manufacturing activities in the developing countries. Although such an estimate is clearly far from perfect, as McMillan himself points out, it does provide a scale by which to measure the importance of various sectors.

Table 6.6 illustrates that by far the largest part of CMEA capital investment is in the mining industry and the development and transformation of natural resources (including fishing). Banking may have been underestimated, as the assets of the Moscow Narodny Bank subsidiaries in Singapore and Beirut and of the

Table 6.6 *Estimated value of capital investment, assets, and turnover of CMEA joint ventures (mixed enterprises) in developing countries, end 1978**

Main activity	Capital investment (1)	Assets (2)	Assets of financing establishments (3)	Turnover (4)
			($m)	
Trading	10.8	29.7	—	256.8
Production	36.0	202.5	—	472.4
Resources development	172.8	3,576.4	—	—
Financial services‡	13.2	0.9	671.0	—
Transport	28.8	62.0	—	—
Other services	8.8	30.8	—	—
Total	270.4	3,902.3	—	—

* The figures in columns 3 and 4 are for end of 1977.
† Value of products sold by CMEA countries.
‡ Does not include capital and assets of the Moscow Narodny Bank in Singapore and Beirut nor those of the Iranian-Soviet Bank.
Source: McMillan, 'Growth of External Investments by the Comecon Countries', p. 371.

Iranian-Soviet Bank are not included in the estimates. Transport's capital and assets are relatively significant, but in the trading sector investments are scarce. It should be noted, however, that in Table 6.6 assets represents the *total* capital of mixed enterprises with CMEA participation. This is much higher than CMEA capital in mixed enterprises in the OECD countries ($3,902m as against $474), but CMEA participants in mixed enterprises usually have equal or majority shares in OECD countries, whilst in developing countries they usually have the smallest number of shares. Hence in developing countries the value of capital belonging to CMEA countries has much less significance. McMillan estimated that their investments in mixed enterprises in developing countries were $120m (end 1978), as against $396m invested in OECD countries.

We were not able to estimate a breakdown of the companies to show whether CMEA participation was on a majority, minority, or equal basis, or even whether they were wholly owned by CMEA countries. But we do know that the Tehran, Singapore, and Beirut banks are wholly Soviet-owned and that Romania's shareholding in the Egyptian-Romanian Bank is 49 per cent. It may well be that the Soviet transport companies located in the Philippines and Thailand are 100 per cent Soviet-owned as they usually are in the OECD countries.

In the documents we consulted, only the Romanian ones indicated the breakdown by country of the share of capital in the mixed enterprises. In the majority of cases the Romanian share is slightly less than 50 per cent, but in mining enterprises, where capital is usually of paramount importance, the Romanian share is very small: 2.5 per cent in Minfergi Nimba in Guinea, and 5 per cent in Somifer (iron ore prospecting) in Gabon. Furthermore, in 1978, the Polish share in the Industrie Chimique Senegalaise was only 5 per cent.

It would clearly be worthwhile to carry out further investigations in this area. The CMEA share of fixed capital may indeed be insignificant, but the CMEA countries' impact on developing countries via trade relations may be very important.

In order to expand, the mixed enterprises in developing countries obviously need major financial support. They appear in the main to get such support either from Soviet banks or from the Egyptian-Romanian Bank. For a long time, financial support was provided by the London-based Moscow Narodny Bank, but after the creation in 1963 of the Beirut subsidiary the Middle East no longer had to rely on London. Despite the civil war, this subsidiary was functioning successfully at the end of 1978, financing the export of Soviet industrial products to the Middle East.[5]

In 1971, a subsidiary of the Moscow Narodny Bank was opened in Singapore to facilitate the development of Soviet banking activities in South-East Asia and Australia. Another subsidiary of the Moscow Narodny Bank was also created: the Monab Nominees Pte., Limited.[6] Due to financial activities prompted by defaults on loans[7] the subsidiary bought land in Singapore and Hong Kong, but some observers believe that the object of this move was to acquire important shares which the Soviets would not otherwise have been able to obtain. In this transaction, the Monab Nominees Pte., Limited acted as an intermediary for the Soviet Union.[8]

In addition, capital investments by CMEA countries in developing countries are facilitated because of the latter's balance of payments problems. As a rule, rather than export capital, CMEA countries reinvest profits and raise loans in the developing countries to buy shares in mixed enterprises.[9]

Mixed enterprises as a form of inter-governmental cooperation

Inter-governmental cooperation agreements and bilateral joint comissions

As a survey on CMEA mixed enterprises located in developing countries progressed, it was decided to investigate some of the reasons as to why these enterprises appeared in one country rather than another. The factor which was studied in most detail was the level of the bilateral economic relations between the CMEA and the relevant developing country.

Initially, we compare the data on the location of CMEA mixed enterprises in developing countries (see Table 6.2) with the economic, scientific, and technical agreements signed by the same countries between 1978 and 1983. From the slightly more detailed information we have on African countries it seems that inter-governmental cooperation agreements precede the creation of mixed enterprises. The Soviet Union signed such agreements with Angola. Madagascar, Morocco, and Mozambique; Romania with Gabon, Zaire, and Burundi; Bulgaria with Morocco; and Hungary with Nigeria prior to the establishment of mixed enterprises.[10] For some other countries, however, cooperation agreements are not necessarily followed by the creation of mixed enterprises, which may be due to lack of practical cooperation after the signing of a formal agreement as in the case of Egypt and Czechoslovakia, Gabon and the Soviet Union, Libya and the Soviet Union, Libya and Poland, Mozambique and the GDR, and Nigeria and the GDR.

Our conclusions on this topic can only be tentative, however, and further research is clearly required.

Where such inter-governmental cooperation agreements were signed it was usual for the two parties to set up a joint commission to encourage contacts at a higher level.[11] The list of these joint commissions is incomplete but they appear to work intensively[12] and to have the following common characteristics:

(a) Where there is a joint commission, there are almost always mixed enterprises. The exceptions appear to be Algeria-Hungary, Angola-Poland, Cameroon-GDR, and Libya-Czechoslovakia.

(b) These joint commissions appear to be concerned, amongst other

Table 6.7   *Examples of consortia in developing countries with CMEA participation*

Host country	Partners	Project	Year	Conditions
Argentina[a]	Energomashexport (Soviet Union) Tauro (Argentina)	Hydroelectric power station (1,890 Kwh) on Salto Grande	1981	14 Kaplan Soviet turbines; Soviet loan of $50m over 15 years at 4 per cent
Brazil[b]	Electrosol, Skoda Export (Czechoslovakia) Deutsche Babcock (FRG)	Thermal station (250 MW) at Jorge Lacerda		Deutsche Babcock DM 140m (30 per cent of total cost)
Peru[c]	Soviet Union Peru	Hydroelectric power station, irrigation project	Agreement, 1980	Total cost $1bn, Soviet share $300m; long-term consortium
Algeria[d]	Romanergo (Romania) Sonagther (Algeria)	Le Fahiha dam (100 million m³ 32 mn m³ at Willaya of Mascara to irrigate Habra	Agreement, 18 April 1979	'Grouping' (imprecise legal form)
Algeria[e]	Marubani Corp., Hitachi Shipbuilding and Engineering (Japan) Polimex-Cekop (Poland) Sonatrach (Algeria)	Two phosphate plants (sulphuric acid, phosphoric acid, fertilizers) in Annaba and Tebessa	Agreement, January 1979	Total cost Y80m or $400m: Japan Y52bn, Poland Y12bn, Algeria Y16bn
Angola[f]	Soviet Union Brazil Portugal Angola	Dam on the Quanza south of Luanda for the irrigation of 400,000 ha; power station of 500,000 KW	Agreement, January 1979	
Libya[g]	Deutsche Babcock and two other Western firms	Desalinization plant for the station of Homs	1978	

Ethiopia[h]	Budimex (Poland) FIM-Ivan Milutovic (Yugoslavia) VEB Textimaprojekt (GDR) and other foreign firms	Textile plant with capacity of 20mn metres	Agreement November 1980
Nigeria[i]	Poland Cuba Soviet Union	Sugar plant	Agreement, July 1981
India[j]	Hungary (leader of consortium)	Aluminium plant in Korba with capacity of 200,000 t/annum	(Around 1975)

Sources:
(a) *Geopolitica*, June 1980, p. 68.
(b) *Promotion of Trade through Industrial Co-operation: Organisation and Management of Tripartite Co-operation: Western Enterprises' Practice in the Building of Therman Energy Power Station*. Note by Committee for Development, Trade Secretariat, Economic Commission for Europe. United Nations. TRADE/R.451, 6 October 1982, pp. 8, 10, 11.
(c) *East–West Trade News*, 30 April 1980, p. 3.
(d) *Marches Tropicaux*, 27 April 1980.
(e) *Marches Tropicaux*, 12 January 1979.
(f) *Marches Tropicaux*, 5 February 1982, p. 339; also *Marches Tropicaux*, 20 November 1981. Soviet Union is chief contractor.
(g) *Promotion of Trade through Industrial Co-operation*, p. 11.
(h) *Marches Tropicaux*, 14 November 1980, p. 3045.
(i) *Handel Zagraniczny*, No. 7 (1981), p. 39.
(j) A. Bokor, 'Know-how, Engineering and Expertise: Currency Earners by Hungarian Aluminium Industry, *Magyar Aluminium*, Nos. 3–4 (1975), pp. 86–8, cited by Agota Dezsenyi-Guellete, 'L'Industrie de L'Aluminium en Hongrie: Co-operation ou Autonomie?' *Revue d'Etudes Comparatives Est–Ouest*, June 1983, p. 156.

things, with the functioning of the mixed enterprises. For instance, the joint Moroccan-Soviet commission deals mainly with fishing, and the joint Gabon-Romanian commission is concerned with mining, with Romania, as the only CMEA partner, holding a 5 per cent share in the mixed enterprise Somifer.

Consortia as a form of cooperation similar to mixed enterprises

Another topic which presents itself for future research is the relationship between project consortia and mixed enterprises. According to UN terminology, a consortium, created for the building of an industrial plant, can be considered a co-enterprise if it is constituted as a collective firm based on the principle of risk and profit making. On the other hand, it is not considered to be a co-enterprise if it is based on a contract which does not include this clause.[13] According to UN experts, however, the structure of management frequently changes as a project progresses from the tendering into the negotiating phase and again into the execution phase.[14]

The overview of consortia (and other forms of cooperation) in Table 6.7 prompts the questions as to whether they are mixed enterprises or exist merely as a form of cooperation in the execution of a project, and whether they constitute a step towards mixed enterprises or are something totally different. For example, there is the *de facto* consortium which exists in Brazil for the building of the Jorge Iacerda power station and which has as its main partners Deutsche Babcock and Skoda Export. They do not legally form a consortium but have acted as such all along.[15] Officially, Deutsche Babcock was the 'sub contractor' for Skoda Export on a contract involving DM140m. According the provision of the trade agreement between Brazil and Czechoslovakia regarding the payments for Skoda Export turbogenerating sets, Deutsche Babcock was to play the 'silent' role in the consortium, but it later became apparent that Deutsche Babcock was acting as a sub-contractor.[16]

In other instances, *de facto* mixed enterprise consortia may be established. Although we have no details on the agreement signed by Peru and the Soviet Union to build a hydroelectric power station and to carry out irrigation (a $300m investment), we do know that it is a long-term project in which risk and profit sharing has its place.

A further study is therefore necessary to determine the true legal aspect of the other consortia in which there is participation from both East and West. It would be interesting to know the legal status of a plant or an electric power station once it is built. In general, although the host country usually takes over the plant and pays for the outstanding debt, this may not have happened in Argentina, Algeria, and Angola. Comparing Tables 6.1 and 6.7, we can also see that in Ethiopia, Nigeria, and India such plants may have been converted into mixed enterprises. Further research should clarify this point.

CMEA investments and their contribution to the creation of mixed enterprises

CMEA countries' investments in the Third World account for a large part of their economic activities. Between 1948 and 1978, CMEA countries signed agreements for the creation of 3,560 industrial and other projects; 2,685 of them had actually been established by the middle of 1979.[17] The Soviet Union had 998 such projects of which 555 had been established[18] by 1 January 1979.

It is very difficult, however, in view of the lack of data on investments to know the extent to which these projects proceed to the establishment of mixed enterprises, compared with the degree to which they merely signify technical assistance. Usually, investments in mixed enterprises where there is a CMEA country's participation are kept secret, but in order to obtain some preliminary results we investigated CMEA countries' investments in Africa over the past five years (1979–83). We then compared the results with data on CMEA mixed enterprises.

Our results must be read with several qualifications, since our list on CMEA mixed enterprises in Africa is far from exhaustive and such enterprises are subject to frequent changes. In addition, although we included the most significant investments, we have no information on their legal status. From the data shown in Tables 6.1 and 6.8 it appears that between 1979 and 1983 there have been 218 investment projects completed or about to be completed in Africa, but only seventy mixed enterprises. The Soviet Union is involved in approximately 40 per cent of these investment projects but in only 20 per cent of mixed enterprises.

Furthermore, the Soviet Union has 70 per cent and the other CMEA countries 51 per cent of their investment projects in pro-socialist countries such as Algeria, Angola, Congo Brazzaville,

Table 6.8 *Overview of recent CMEA investments in Africa, 1979–1983*

Countries	Bulgaria	Czecho-slovakia	GDR	Hungary	Poland	Romania	Soviet Union	Total
Algeria	—	—	1	8	2	—	8	19
Angola	—	—	—	—	—	—	6	6
Benin	—	1	—	—	—	—	—	1
Congo (People's Republic of)	—	—	—	—	—	—	7	7
Egypt	—	—	—	—	—	—	1	1
Ethiopia	—	—	1	—	—	—	6	7
Gabon	—	—	—	—	—	2	3	5
Ghana	—	—	—	—	—	5	1	6
Guinea	—	—	—	—	—	1	—	1
Kenya	—	—	—	8	—	—	—	8
Libya	14	5	—	—	6	1	12	38
Madagascar	—	—	6	1	—	—	10	17
Mali	—	—	—	—	—	—	5	5
Morocco	2	5	—	—	6	7	5	25
Mauritania	—	—	—	—	—	3	1	4
Mozambique	—	—	—	4	—	—	13	17
Nigeria	—	3	4	1	2	—	7	17
Senegal	—	—	—	—	4	—	—	4
Sudan	—	1	—	—	4	3	—	8
Tanzania	1	—	3	—	—	—	—	4
Tunisia	—	—	5	—	—	—	2	7
Zaire	—	—	—	—	—	3	—	3
Zambia	—	1	—	—	—	7	—	8
Total	17	16	20	22	24	32	87	218

Note: Some one hundred projects are to be completed with the assistance of the Soviet Union (*Marches Tropicaux*, 1 January 1982, p. 18).

Libya, Madagascar, Mozambique, and Ethiopia, whilst the figure for CMEA mixed enterprises in Africa is only 21 per cent. From this we can conclude that in their selection of the form of economic relations with African countries, CMEA countries take into account the political stance of these countries. This conclusion is also supported by the inference of both official and non-official sources that one of the aims of socialist investments in developing countries is gradually to reinforce social and economic changes,[19] and it would appear that investment projects are used to serve this purpose. Mixed enterprises, on the other hand, seem to prefer to operate in those countries having more developed market economies, to meet objectives of hard currency sales turnover.

Table 6.9 *Recent investments by CMEA countries in Africa, 1979–1983*

	Investments*	Mixed enterprises †
1. Mining and energy industry		
Non-ferrous metal	2	—
Ore (in general)	6	1
Iron ore	1	2
Lead and zinc ore	2	1
Magnesite	1	—
Gold	2	1
Molybdena	1	—
Tin	1	—
Nickel	2	—
Uranium	1	—
Bauxite and alumina	3	—
Hydrocarbons	1	—
Energy (in general)	1	—
Oil	6	—
Coal	4	1
Electrification	16	—
Nuclear power stations	1	—
Copper ore	4	2
Total	55	8
2. Manufacturing industry		
General	1	1
Metal working	9	—
Machinery	1	—
Machine tools	2	—
Agricultural machinery	3	—
Tractors	2	1
Cars	2	1
Buses	3	—
Electrotechnical industry	3	—
Refrigeration	4	—
Shipbuilding	4	—
Refineries	2	—
Chemicals	1	2
Mineral fertilizers (phosphates)	7	—
Petrochemistry	1	—
Sulphuric acid	1	—
Building	1	—
Building materials	1	—

	*Investments**	*Mixed enterprises* †
Cement	2	—
Sleeper plants	2	—
Printing	1	—
Glass making	1	—
Spare parts	1	—
Wood	2	5
Silos	1	—
Slaughterhouses	2	—
Textiles	7	—
Food	2	—
Fish processing	1	1
Beverages	1	—
Sugar	1	—
Shoes	1	—
Flour milling	—	1
Pharmaceuticals	—	1
Total	73	13
3. Agriculture		
Pilot farms	1	—
General	3	1
Soil improvement and irrigation	8	1
Agri-foodstuffs sector	5	1
Industrial crop (cotton)	4	4
Soja	1	—
Breeding (sheep, hens)	2	3
Pig breeding	1	—
Gum	—	1
Tree nurseries	—	1
Maize	—	1
Total	25	13
4. Natural resources development		
General	—	1
Fisheries	2	8
Total	2	9
5. Prospecting	13	1
6. Construction		
General	1	3
Housing	8	—
Engineering and consulting	1	2
Total	10	5

	Investments*	Mixed enterprises †
7. Transport and telecommunications		
General	4	—
Railroads	6	—
Marine transport	2	—
Harbours	9	—
Road transport	4	1
Telephones	1	—
Air transport	1	—
Gas pipelines	3	—
Oil pipelines	1	—
Total	31	1
8. Services		
Research institutes and schools	8	—
Hospitals	15	1
Health services	1	—
Veterinary hospitals	1	1
Hotels	1	1
Total	26	3
9. Trading only	—	7
Total, all sectors	235	60

* Certain investments appearing in this table have been counted several times as they concern several sectors.

† The statistics on investments and mixed enterprises were drawn up independently. Investment figures are for 1979–83 and include completed projects. Figures for mixed enterprises start in 1970 and include all enterprises mentioned. Some investments became mixed enterprises but we chose to leave them out in order not to create confusion. Certain African countries where mixed enterprises were identified (Burundi, Cameroon, Central Republic of Africa, Ivory Coast, Liberia, Sierra Leone, Somalia, Zimbabwe) do not appear in this table showing investments in 1979–1983. This is because mixed enterprises created before 1979 are shown in Table 6.1 and also because there are gaps in our survey.

These conclusions, however, need to be modified in view of important differences between Table 6.1 and Table 6.8 for CMEA countries other than the Soviet Union. For example, in the case of Romania, there is virtually an equal number of mixed enterprises and investment projects in Africa. Consequently, it is not unreasonable to conclude that the official Romanian line is as strongly in favour of creating mixed enterprises as of participating in investment projects. On the other hand, whereas the GDR, Hungary, and Poland have a more or less equal number of investment projects (see Table 6.8), Table 6.1 shows no mixed enterprise at all for the GDR and far more for Poland than Hungary. The negative result for the GDR is probably due to secrecy, since according to personal information obtained by the author, the GDR has the same number of mixed enterprises in Africa as Czechoslovakia or Hungary, which have five each. Table 6.9 gives further information of CMEA investments and mixed enterprises in Africa by industrial sector. The number of mixed enterprises is obviously lower since the sample chosen for investments is not the most representative.

Mixed enterprises, compared with investment projects, are strikingly scarce in the sectors of heavy industry (mining and energy), manufacturing industry, and services and transport, although pro-socialist countries appear to attract more of this type of investment. A reason for the absence of direct investments by CMEA countries in developing countries is suggested by the data in Table 6.6. For example, although there are $3.7b of assets held in mixed enterprises concerned with heavy industry (resources development and production) more often than not CMEA participation is as a minor shareholder for example Romania's 5 per cent shareholding in Somifer (Gabon) and 2.5 per cent shareholding in Minfergi Nimba (Guinea)).

Low-cost direct investments are also probably more abundant in such areas as agriculture, the wood industry, and small-investment trading. The fishing industry also appears to have a larger number of mixed enterprises than investments. In spite of the relatively small amount of capital investment, CMEA mixed enterprises appear more likely to be found in production.[20] It is still uncertain, however, by what process an investment becomes a mixed enterprise.

We were not able to obtain any information on the Soviet share in the mining complex in Mfonati (Congo Brazzaville) nor in the lead and gold mines in Congo. Furthermore, the Soviet share in the Cosmos hotel seems to have been sold to a French enterprise. Doubts

Table 6.10 *Trade with countries accepting socialist joint ventures relative to total trade with that area, 1982*

	Africa	Asia	Latin America (%)	Middle East	Total developing countries
Hungary	3.1	66.4	77.7	55.6	45.8
Poland	31.0	60.8	7.7	37.8	30.6
Romania	84.7	72.8	44.6	47.1	55.0
Soviet Union†	47.6	88.3	96.8	45.8	73.3

† Figures for the Soviet Union are for 1981.
Sources: List of appendix (summarised in Table 6.2) and annual statistics on foreign trade published by Comecon countries.
Hungary — *Kulkerskedelmi Statisztikaj Evokonyv, 1982* (Foreign Trade Statistics, 1982). Kosponti Statisztikai Hivatal, Budapest, 12 September 1983, pp. 15–16; Poland — *Rocznik Statystyczny Handlu Zagranicznego, 1983* (Foreign Trade Statistics, 1983). Gowny Urzad Statystyczny Warszawa, 1983, pp. 26–9; Romania — *Annuarul Statistical Reputlicii Socialiste Romania, 1983*, Bucharest, pp. 250–3; Soviet Union — Fiansy i Statistika (ed.).*Vnesnjaja Torgovlja USSR v 1981 g. Statisticheskij Sbornik* (Foreign Trade Statistics, 1981), Moscow, 1982, pp. 10–14.

also remain as to the Soviet capital share in the Prefab Concrete Factory in Ghana and in Mozambique.

Mixed enterprises and trade between CMEA countries and developing countries

As part of this current survey, it was decided to investigate the impact of mixed enterprises on trade between CMEA countries and the developing countries. Table 6.10 shows the results of our investigation of the relation between socialist multinationals and CMEA trade with developing countries for defined locations in 1982. These percentages clearly vary according to the CMEA country and the location of the socialist multinational. For example, trade and mixed enterprises are most closely related in the case of the Soviet Union, followed by Romania. The geographical area of mixed enterprise location also plays a very important part. In Africa, for example, the CMEA countries appear to behave differently, with Romania encouraging the creation of mixed enterprises and trade, while

Hungary is far more restrained. In Latin America, however, the opposite appears to be the case, with Hungarian enterprises playing a far more important role than their Romanian counterparts. In Asia and the Middle East there appears to be more consistency across all of the named socialist countries. In the case of Poland the overall link between mixed enterprises and trade appears to be very small although Poland is active in creating mixed enterprises. Clearly, these topics warrant further research.

We also compared the location of mixed enterprises with the various developing countries' trade balances, since it was concerned that a trade balance in favour of CMEA countries might encourage the creation of mixed enterprises, especially if trade relations are regulated by clearing agreements. We analysed the respective 1982 trade balances for the four CMEA countries, cited in Table 6.10 (Hungary, Poland, Romania and the Soviet Union) and in the majority of cases it was found that in those developing countries where there were trade balance surpluses in favour of CMEA countries, there were also mixed enterprises. This clearly requires further research to investigate the possible causality between these two factors.

In some instances the surpluses were insignificant, as in the cases of the Hungary-Lebanon, Romania-Lebanon and Hungary-Iran trade balances. Some mixed enterprises also exist where there are trade balance deficits, as in the cases of Hungary-Brazil, Romania-Iran, and the Soviet Union-Argentina; the Soviet Union has the most mixed enterprises in developing countries where it has a trade balance deficit. Again the reasons for this are suggested as topics for further research.[21]

Conclusion

Having studied CMEA mixed enterprises in developing countries, a major question arises: is there a deliberate policy being applied across the board? The answer would appear to be in the negative, since there is no evidence of a common CMEA policy in this field. In several developing countries the mixed enterprises may even behave as competitors. Such competition does not encourage a common policy for the creation of mixed enterprises, as has been stressed by a Polish expert.[22] However, several Eastern European experts agree that mixed enterprises are a modern form of economic activity that ensures long-term trade stability and encourages mutually profitable economic relations.[23]

It does not appear that maximum profitability is the main criterion influencing the establishment and development of CMEA mixed enterprises in developing countries. Priority is given to certain economic activities such as natural resources development (including agricultural development, forestry, and fishing), trading and final assembly of goods as well as manufacturing industries. Then come the activities which are CMEA specialities: pharmaceuticals and buses (Hungary), mining, textiles, and food products (Poland), electronics and machinery (Czechoslovakia and the GDR). In general, therefore, it appears that CMEA countries offer their know-how and expertise, plus a well-tested, relatively unsophisticated technology which corresponds to the nature of developing countries' needs, through the medium of mixed enterprises. In many of these sectors, however, it may take some time to move into profit and obtain a positive return from investment. It is interesting to note, therefore, that although CMEA countries are in favour of exploiting natural resources, they do not seem able or willing to invest the necessarily huge capital. When they are willing to invest, they would rather do it in the form of low-interest-bearing loan, especially in the case of pro-socialist developing countries. Apart from military aid, political criteria appear to be paramount in this instance. It is also interesting to note that CMEA mixed enterprises sometimes behave like their market economy counterparts in developing countries. In certain cases they are compelled to do so, as in Brazil, where all contracts for the provision of heavy equipment are put out to tender,[24] and in Mauritania, where the creation of mixed enterprises was made a condition of operating in the fisheries. CMEA countries also appear to prefer to have the government of the host developing country or a state institution as their partner in a mixed enterprise venture, but they are sometimes obliged to accept private firms as partners and one also finds cases where there is participation by a Western multinational.

A final question to be considered is: what is the future of CMEA mixed enterprises in developing countries? The overall trend appears to be in favour of these enterprises, since there seem to be few ideological obstacles against operating alongside capitalist multi-nationals when CMEA economic, political, and commercial interests are at stake. Only the rules and risks involved in a market economy account for a possible reluctance to establish more of these mixed enterprises, although a Polish expert has acknowledged this problem and maintains that they are accepted. Yet at the same time, there appears to be only a limited spirit of enterpreneurship in the CMEA countries.

For example, Romania planned a huge increase in the number of its mixed enterprises in the years 1975–80, but in reality they were reduced from sixty in 1975 to forty-five in 1976.[25] This contraction underlines the dificulties experienced by mixed enterprises, namely:

— the political and economic instability of the developing countries;
— the difficulty in obtaining reliable data before committing investments;
— the difficulty in securing sufficient capital and qualified employees.

There is also evidence that Polish participation in the Senegalese chemical industry has been reduced.[26]

Although these difficulties exist, they must not, however, be exaggerated, since lack of experience is often only transitory while real advantages can be permanent. CMEA countries can use reinvested profits and local loans, they have a good position in clearing agreements, and they are competitive on price and credit facilities. It would appear that countries like the Soviet Union have increased the number of their mixed enterprises in developing countries and this trend could well be confirmed in the future. The same may be true of other CMEA countries.

Notes and references

1. Carl H. McMillan, 'Growth of External Investments by the Comecon Countries', *The World Economy*, 2, No. 3 (September 1979), pp. 363–86; McMillan, 'Soviet Investment in the Industrial Western Economies and in the Developing Economies of the Third World', in *Soviet Economy in Time of Change*, Joint Economic Committee, 96th Congress, 1st Session, Vol.2, October 1979, US Government Printing Office, Washington DC, 1979, pp. 625–47.
2. McMillan 'Growth of External Investments by the Comecon Countries', p. 366. The low figure for the GDR reflects the lack of data rather than the absence of activities.
3. Ibid, p. 366, and McMillan, 'Soviet Investment in the Industrial Western Economies', p. 630.
4. McMillan, 'Growth of External Investments by the Comecon Countries', p. 370.

5. S.T. Rabin,'Soviet-owned Banks in Europe: Their Development and Contribution to Trade with the West, unpublished doctoral thesis quoted by McMillan, 'Soviet Investment in the Industrial Western Economies', p. 639.
6. The date of the subsidiary's creation remains unknown.
7. The Singapore MNB subsidiary's difficulties appeared in 1976. Some investments in a casino in Bangkok and property speculations turned sour. The subsidiary had $100m-worth of bad debts, which provoked a flurry of commentaries in the West (McMillan, 'Soviet Investment in the Industrial Western Economies', p. 639).
8. Ibid., p. 639, note.
9. McMillan, 'Growth of External Investments by the Comecon Countries' p. 372.
10. *Marches Tropicaux*, 1978–83.
11. Soviet-Moroccan cooperation is organized by the Grand Commission (*Marches Tropicaux*, 19 September and 14 November 1980). There is also a large Franco-Soviet Commission.
12. Certain joint commissions are very dynamic: the joint Madagascar-Soviet Commission held five meetings between 1980 and 1984 (*Marches Tropicaux*, 19 September to 14 November 1980).
13. *Guide to International Contracts Drafting between Parties United to Carry Out a Specific Project*, ECT/TRADE/731, New York, 1979. Quoted by *Promotion of Trade through Industrial Co-operation: Organisation and Management of Tripartite Co-operation: Western Enterprises' Practice in the Building of Thermal Energy Power Station*, Note by Committee for Development, Trade Secretariat, Economic Commission for Europe, United Nations, TRADE/R.451, 6 October 1982, p. 7.
14. Ibid., p. 7.
15. Ibid., p. 8.
16. Ibid., p. 14.
17. Mieczyslaw Gulcz and Bohdan Gluckman, 'Industrial Investment Assistance: The Socialist Countries' Approach to the Third World, in F.E.I. Hamilton and G.J.R. Linge (eds.), *Spatial Analysis: Industry and the Industrial Environment*, Vol. 11, *International Industrial Systems*, John Wiley & Sons Ltd., 1981, p. 215.
18. Ibid, p. 217. Out of the 998 projects, 429 were in production and manufacturing, 147 in agriculture, 94 in transport and telecommunications, 65 in research and prospecting, 238 in culture, education, and health, and 25 in other activities.
19. Gulcz and Gluckman, 'Industrial Investment Assistance', p. 218.
20. We deliberately classified the firms concerned solely with trading separately so as to stress the difference with mixed enterprises in industrialized countries, where trading prevails.
21. Information on trade balances was drawn from the same sources as the data shown in Table 6.10.
22. Aleksander Jung, 'Wielostronne Spolki Firm Soojalistycznych Wakrajach Rozwijajacych sie' (Socialist Mixed Enterprises in Developing Countries), *Handel Zagraniczny*, No. 3 (1981), p. 27.
23. Adine Dan,'Mixed Trading Firms',*Bucharest UEAC*, November 1981, in Romanian, June 1981, p. 3.

24. R. Acciaris, 'Observations on Trade Relations between Brazil and East European Socialist Countries between 1970–1979, unpublished paper, Université Paris III.

25. See *Romania Liberia*, 11 June 1975, and *Romanian Foreign Trade Magazine*, No. 2 (1976), pp. 13–15.

26. Ciech had a 10 per cent share in the Senegalese chemical industry in 1976 and a 5 per cent share in 1978, but in 1979 it announced its withdrawal (see *Financing of Tripartite East-West Industrial Co-operation in the Mediterranean Area — Politics, Practices and Constraints*, Committee on Trade Development, 31st Session, Economic Commission for Europe, 6–10 December 1982, United Nations, TRADE/R.454, 27 October 1982, p. 32).

7 Conclusion

Geoffrey Hamilton

In the introduction to this book we outlined the main characteristics of a multinational corporation. Having now examined the activities of companies from the Soviet Union and Eastern Europe in several European countries and in the developing world, we can attempt to determine whether they can be seriously compared with the companies we more commonly refer to as multinationals.

It should be stressed at this point that there are appreciable differences between the socialist countries in their operations in the West. They should not be treated as an homogeneous bloc of countries even though they share the same Marxist-Leninist ideology. Each country, after all, possesses separate and different laws concerning its external commercial activities. Also some socialist countries manage their own economies in contrasting ways. For example the economy of the Soviet Union is centrally planned, whereas the Hungarian economy, while remaining essentially socialist, has a more decentralized and market-orientated structure which gives local enterprises greater autonomy from the State. These characteristics, in turn, account for the differences in the way in which each country's external economic relations are organized. It is therefore dangerous to make general conclusions which cover all the countries of Eastern Europe. This being said, however, we shall now try to state the common features of these companies uncovered by the country case studies.

Size

In this section we are looking at the size of these firms, the overall investment of the socialist countries in those countries surveyed and whether the firms examined displayed any evidence of the dynamism hinted at by a number of authors, elsewhere, which could suggest that they are following the same path taken by today's mammoth multinationals such as Ford, IBM or Nestlé decades ago.

The evidence, however, points to a very different direction to the one taken by the West's multinationals. Investment by the socialist countries in our sample of countries was tiny in relation to Western investors. In the United Kingdom, for example, the assets of firms from the socialist countries represented only 0.2 per cent of total net assets of overseas companies in the British private sector. In Austria, only 1.0 per cent of total nominal capital under direct foreign influence was owned by socialist countries. In the United Kingdom the annual turnover of these socialist companies in 1979 was £1.15b which, measured against the special dividend of £1b paid by Ford UK to its American parent in 1981, shows the small scale of commercial activity of these countries in the United Kingdom.

Moreover, the size of these firms from the Soviet Union and Eastern Europe appeared almost universally small. In West Germany, Knirsch found this characteristic to be the case with the majority of firms he examined. Similarly in the United Kingdom, the average total fixed assets of firms was only £3/4m in 1979. In Sweden, the assets of socialist enterprises were found by Hill to be even smaller than those in the United Kingdom. The same finding was reached in the Austrian survey, with most of the firms possessing an average capital of only Sch.1.5m. The smallness of these companies can be further illustrated by looking at the number of workers they employ. Only 3,200 Austrians were employed in socialist firms in 1981 out of 247,000 employees working in companies under direct foreign influence.

Of course, both Hill's and Knirsch's studies showed that the majority of socialist investments were quite recent. It might be argued therefore that these companies' intention was to start out on a small scale and, after acquiring necessary experience and resources, grow and expand. While our studies cannot disprove this hypothesis, Hill found, after directly questioning the managers of several socialist firms in the United Kingdom, no evidence of any strategy to expand their present activities.

Motives for investment and nature of activity

All the case studies show that the reason for the establishment of socialist enterprises in Europe was to boost the trade of products already made in the Soviet Union and Eastern Europe.[1] Consequently, the vast majority of firms are found in the trade related sector of the economy. Of the 157 companies analysed in the West German study, eighty-two (52 per cent) were trading companies, twenty-six (17 per cent) service enterprises, forty-six (29 per cent) agencies, and significantly only three firms were registered as production enterprises. Similar findings arose in the United Kingdom, Sweden and Austria surveys. The role of these trading companies was to assemble and market products made in the socialist countries and provide customers with such things as after-sales services. The alternative to the setting up of these trading firms to market the products of the socialist countries is independent commercial agencies or import firms. The main advantage of doing this task by themselves is that it avoids having to pay a commission to such agencies. Indeed Hill's research found that all the companies queried were strongly of the opinion that their presence in the West enabled them to market their socialist manufactured products more effectively than selling through agents.

By improving their trade with the West these countries earn badly-needed Western currency which allows them to purchase raw materials and manufactured goods from the West. As Knirsch pointed out, the shortage of hard Western currency, which had led to many socialist countries becoming indebted to Western banks, was the principal cause for the emergence of these companies in the 1970s.

One of the few exceptions to this trading company model of socialist enterprise which cropped up in the Austrian, United Kingdom and Swedish surveys was Tungsram, the Hungarian producer of such things as lightbulbs and car headlamps. It owns factories and operates in joint-ventures in Western Europe and the United States as well as in some developing countries and is Hungary's biggest earner of foreign currency. Under Hungarian economic reforms it advertises widely in the West. Recently, its subsidiary in Cork, which at one stage was producing twenty million bulbs a year for the European market, closed as a result of slump in demand in the United Kingdom market, with a total loss of some £5m. This led to the restructuring of the company as a whole with the selling of certain acquisitions and the laying off of 2,000 of its Hungarian workforce of 25,000.

This 'red multinational' is, however, an exception to the trading-firm model in Western Europe. An explanation for its existence is that it is one of the 'old-holdings' left over from the time of the Austro-Hungarian monarchy and the period between the two world wars.

Unlike all the other Austrian multinationals of that era, it was not nationalized after 1945. Thus it constitutes a special category of capital investment by the socialist countries.

The fact that there is so little investment in manufacturing in the West by socialist companies is perhaps unsurprising. As Stanley Paliwoda declared in his study of trade and investment between East and West: 'it is difficult to envisage these socialist enterprises investing in manufacturing plant overseas so long as they have a captive market, low cost labour and an export capability with a high value to weight ratio, with further market protection arising from their monopolistic situation in foreign trade'.[2] With none of the market pressures of competition to bother them, Eastern firms can stay at home. We shall return to the reasons why firms from socialist countries are reluctant to internationalize their production.

Thus, if one believes, as described in the introduction, that a multinational manufactures abroad either to benefit from lower labour costs or to avoid high tariff barriers then the companies founded by the socialist countries have a rather different motivation. There is a total lack of evidence of socialist companies adopting a multinational strategy to manufacture products or parts of products in different countries.

Of course, those who argue that the West's own multinationals branched into manufacturing after starting initially as trading enterprises can speculate that these socialist enterprises may do the same, but there are reasons why such a prospect is hard to visualize.

The foreign trade organization and the state-trading monopoly

According to the studies, the vast majority of companies from the Soviet Union and Eastern Europe in the West are owned by the country's foreign trade organization (FTO). Either the FTO sets up a wholly owned company in the West like, for example, the case of Skorimpex Rind Ltd. in the United Kingdom, owned by Skorimpex of Poland, or the FTO enters into a joint venture with a Western-based company as in the case of another Polish FTO, Anglo-Dal, which owns 50 per cent of the Ridpath Pek Ltd., a company marketing meat products in the United Kingdom. Sometimes, several FTOs combine to set up a company like the British Umo Plant Ltd.

which is jointly owned by Tractorexport, Autoexport, Mashinoexport, Techmashimport, Energomashexport and Sudoimport, FTOs from the Soviet Union. Umo Plant Ltd. markets and services construction and transport equipment.

The most relevant point about the FTOs is that they are legally separate from the local enterprise in the Soviet Union or Eastern Europe which makes the products. Thus there would have to be a major policy change in these countries for the FTOs to invest directly in manufacturing companies in the West.

The reason for this separation between production and trade is that foreign trade in all socialist countries is the monopoly of the state. No individual enterprise can engage in export or import activities unless the state has given it the legal right to do so. The state monopoly of foreign trade was established in the Soviet Union soon after the 1917 October revolution by a Decree of the Council of People's Commissars of 22 April 1918. The Decree stated:[3]

> All foreign trade shall be nationalized. Commercial transactions, both the purchase and sale of all kinds of products of the mining industry or manufacturing industries, of agriculture, etc., with foreign governments and individual commercial enterprises abroad shall be executed in the name of the Russian Republic by organs specially empowered thereto. All commercial transaction with foreign countries, both import and export, are forbidden except by these organs.

In the other socialist countries of Eastern Europe the State monopoly of foreign trade was introduced shortly after the establishment of a socialist form of government.

It is not accurate to say however that these FTOs are wholly State controlled. From the legal point of view the FTO is a separately defined legal entity and from the economic point of view, the FTO is self supporting. None the less the State, through the Ministry of Foreign Trade supervises the activities of FTOs who are ultimately responsible to their Ministry and operate under State-controlled charters.

The major functions of an FTO are:

(a) the conclusion and fulfilment of transactions with foreign organizations and firms for the export and import of goods;
(b) placing orders and signing contracts with the enterprises supplying the export goods;

(c) the purchase of import goods for their country's enterprises;
(d) the organization of technical services for the equipment, machinery and instruments sold abroad;
(e) the study of foreign markets with a view to making the best use of market conditions when purchasing or selling goods.

Usually the FTO needs authorization from the Ministry of Foreign Trade when it imports or exports a particular good. The individual enterprise if it wishes to import a particular good must do so through the relevant FTO. Equally, it does not have the legal authority to export to foreign markets. In practice, however, while a FTO acts as a buying and selling organization on behalf of producing and consuming enterprises and conducts foreign trade, actual purchasing decisions are normally made by the users, i.e. the local enterprises. However, these enterprises do not participate as parties to foreign trade contracts.

Given this separation between the producing and trade functions and the role of the FTOs it is at this point useful to remind ourselves of one of the key characteristics of the Western multinational corporation: its multinationally integrated production system. The multinational corporation does everything under its own roof; it produces, trades and markets its products across countries but under its own corporate strategy which is often fixed at its headquarters. On the other hand, most of the companies from the Soviet Union and Eastern Europe that operate in the West are legally and commercially separate from the enterprises of these countries. The FTO does not act like the corporate headquarters of a multinational because it is not a part of the enterprise in the East.

Recently, a tendency has been observed for the number of FTOs in the socialist countries to increase as a result of the need to handle a greater number of specific products for exports. Nevertheless, in many cases the FTO has still responsibility for a variety of products made in several completely separate enterprises. It is because the FTO is not part of the individual enterprise in the socialist countries that their firms in the West are not part of a multinationally integrated production system. The exceptions are where the individual enterprises in the socialist countries have their *own* FTO or where they directly export to Western markets.

Evidence of multinationally integrated production systems under the control of socialist enterprises with commercial activities in the West

We would argue that there would be a greater tendency for multinationals from the socialist countries to develop if their indigenous enterprises organized their production and distribution outside their country or origin and in one or several Western countries. As we have seen the FTOs in the Soviet Union and the Eastern European countries represent an obstaclt to development of such multinationally integrated production system since they are often separate from the enterprise in the socialist country. However, as we have indicated earlier, not all socialist countries organize their external commercial activities in the same way. In the Soviet Union no enterprise has its own FTO nor is permitted to participate as a party to foreign-trade contracts. In Hungary, in contrast, enterprises are allowed to carry out foreign-trade activities. In 1984 about 250 enterprises, including over 200 industrial enterprises, were authorized to engage directly in foreign-trade activities. Only forty-four of these 250 authorized enterprises were foreign-trade companies. In Poland the new economic reform introduced in 1981–2 encourage Polish enterprises to export their products directly to Western markets. As an incentive to these Polish enterprises, the new reform allows the enterprises to retain a considerable proportion of their export earning (up to 50 per cent) for the purpose of export expansion. These funds may be freely utilized for the purchase abroad of raw materials and other inputs to increase export production. Thus in the Polish and Hungarian cases many of the companies set up in the West are either partially or totally owned by an indigenous enterprise from the respective socialist country. In these cases, although they are only involved in marketing the products of the company from the socialist country, it could be argued that they form part of a multinationally integrated production system.

The fact that the institutional separation between production and trade in the socialist countries is in the process of becoming blurred is confirmed by recent evidence from the Soviet Union. The Soviet Union has argued that the separation of trade and production does not mean that there is a lack of contact between industry and foreign trade. On the contrary, they argue, industrial enterprises and FTOs work in close contact and act in concert. However, in practice, this system has imposed bureaucratic obstacles not only in exporting goods of industrial enterprises but in supplying them with Western imports. Long waits for Western imported products are common,[4] and industrial enterprises in the Soviet Union have no incentive to export because they have to produce to a higher standard while they themselves receive limited benefits from sales abroad.

It is perhaps not surprising to note that the export of manufactured products from the Soviet Union is rather insignificant in comparison to its exports of commodities like oil and gas.

As part of an effort, in the words of the new President Mikhail Gorbachëv, 'to improve substantially the whole system of incentives for enterprises to produce for export markets',[5] the Foreign Trade Ministries are being reorganized so that they are in closer contact with the industrial enterprises. For example Afto export, the foreign trade organization in charge of the export of motor vehicles, notably the Lada car, will become part of the Automobile Industry Ministry. The car plant, therefore, at Togliattigrad will be more involved in export efforts. Time will tell whether these reforms prove successful. The evidence from Poland, however, where more ambitious reforms have been introduced does not augur well for the success of the Soviet initiative. In 1981–2 Poland introduced new reforms to allow their companies to trade on their own. The aim was to force exporters to innovate and improve efficiency by bringing them into direct contact with foreign competition. But the results of a recent Institute of the National Economy (IEN) study show that instead of accepting such new opportunities and directly trading with Western markets and indeed possibly setting up some affiliate in the host country, 75 per cent of the firms surveyed preferred the traditional method of handing over their products to the appropriate FTO.[6] The advantage of these reforms to the individual enterprise is that it gives them the chance to obtain higher profits from trade. But in doing so the company must accept the risk of failing and not having its products sold, a risk which the majority of Polish enterprises to date are unwilling to take.

The absence of red multinationals in the West

This conclusion has argued that on the basis of our country case studies little evidence has been uncovered to suggest that the socialist companies at present in the West are little more than insignificant trading companies with little immediate prospect of developing into part of a multinationally integrated production system. These companies can be called 'red multinationals' but there seems little point in using a concept fashioned in the West to refer to the product of a very different economic system.

Of course it cannot be disproved that these companies might make the transition from trading into production and form part of a multinationally integrated production system with its headquarters in one of the socialist countries. Future research ought to undertake more fieldwork on the motivations of managers of socialist enterprises in the West. It also ought to examine the linkages between the FTOs and the enterprises in the socialist countries to discover to what extent production and trade act in concert. This is a very difficult area of research but one which would uncover fascinating material on the motivations of managers from a socialist economic system.

Given however for the moment the absence of real 'red multi-nationals' we can conclude by asking why the companies from socialist countries have not utilized foreign investment and multi-national production as a means of developing their own economies or their own trade potential. First of all, socialist countries' attitudes towards economic change are risk averse and highly conservative. Secondly, there are ideological constraints stemming from Lenin's critical view of the role of international monopolies in the historic evolution of capitalism which prevent socialist policy-makers considering seriously the multinational option. Thirdly, the eco-nomies of Eastern Europe are not export-led growth economies like Japan. There is no imperative to export manufactured goods in return for raw materials as in the case of the Japanese. Thus multinational production as a means of boosting exports is not a high priority in their economic policy thinking.

Fourthly, there are no obvious groups which can be seen to directly benefit from multinational production in the socialist countries. The socialist firms themselves do not need to work for markets in the way capitalist multinationals have to. They are guaranteed markets in their own countries free from competition. As we have seen above, efforts to change this are under way in many socialist countries. But it is too soon to see whether 'true' socialist multinationals will develop as a result. Finally, Western host countries may be a formidable obstacle to the implantation of socialist productive enterprises in the West as was the case of the French Government when it blocked the bid by Balkancar to buy a local French enterprise.

Until such barriers are removed these companies in the West will remain more 'red herrings' than 'red multinationals'.

Notes

1. The evidence from developing countries leads to a slightly different story. As Zaleski found, information on East European activities in these countries is extremely difficult to obtain. None the less, he found that unlike in Western developed countries these firms' activities are often to be found in manufacturing. However, such evidence has to be treated very cautiously. For it is still uncertain to what extent the term 'manufacturing' is used to refer to assembly work.
2. Stanley J. Paliwoda, 'Multinational Corporations: Trade and Investment Across the East–West Divide', *Managerial and Decision Economics*, 2, No. 4, 1981.
3. Suod Ustanovleniy, 1918, No. 33, p. 432.
4. See P. Cockburn, 'Moscow set to modify trade monopoly', *Financial Times*, 22 October 1985, p. 6.
5. Ibid.
6. 'Poland's exporters still subsidised', *Financial Times*, 30 July 1985.

Index

(Note: the corporate organizations listed in this index are those mentioned in the textual material. Those mentioned only in the tables have not been indexed.)